Mildreds
EASY VEGAN

Mildreds

EASY VEGAN

EXCITING *food*, SIMPLY *cooked*

hamlyn

hamlyn

First published in Great Britain in 2023 by Hamlyn,
an imprint of Octopus Publishing Group Ltd
Carmelite House
50 Victoria Embankment
London EC4Y 0DZ
www.octopusbooks.co.uk

An Hachette UK Company
www.hachette.co.uk

Distributed in the US by Hachette Book Group,
1290 Avenue of the Americas, 4th and 5th Floors
New York, NY 10104

Distributed in Canada by Canadian Manda Group,
664 Annette St, Toronto, Ontario, Canada M6S 2C8

ISBN 978-0-600-63805-6

A CIP catalogue record for this book is available from
the British Library.

Printed and bound in China.

10 9 8 7 6 5 4 3 2 1

Editorial Director: Natalie Bradley
Art Director: Yasia Williams
Design concept and illustrations: Paul Lynch, Tiegan Magill
and Sinead Floyd from SAINT Design
Senior Editor: Leanne Bryan
Copy Editor: Tara O'Sullivan
Photographer: David Loftus
Props Stylist: Agathe Gits
Production Manager: Caroline Alberti

MIX
Paper | Supporting
responsible forestry
FSC® C008047

Contents

introduction

Meet Mildreds

The first Mildreds opened in the heart of London's Soho in 1988 with a mission be a cool, casual restaurant without any meat. Our food is colourful, international, seasonal and, most importantly, tasty. We have a wealth of creativity and well-loved dishes to share with you, as well as plenty of tips and advice for excellent plant-based cooking at home.

soho since '88

Meet *Easy Vegan*

Vegan cooking may feel daunting at first, but this book has been written to make sure plant-based food is accessible, delicious and, of course, EASY. Whether you follow a completely vegan diet or not, you will find these recipes are the perfect way to introduce new ideas into your kitchen. With this book, we want to show you how exciting vegan cooking can be. When you eat these dishes, you will never feel like you are missing out on meat and dairy. Instead, you will be opening yourself up to new ingredients, techniques and experiences.

These recipes are written by our chefs, from our homes to yours. We want to share how we cook in our own time, as busy working people who need to make something nice when they get home after a long day, feed hungry kids in a hurry, whip up a date-night dinner or create a quick, impressive meal for guests at the weekend without spending all day in the kitchen. We cooked all these dishes at home for our friends and loved ones, and nothing made it into the book if it wasn't a hit with them. Of course, we have also included some favourites with our customers at the restaurants, too, while making sure they're all super simple to recreate at home.

HOW TO USE *EASY VEGAN*

To help you feel fully confident and prepared to start cooking amazing vegan food, we've included a **toolkit** of useful and time-saving equipment (see pages 8–9) and a **shopping guide** (see pages 9–13) to help you understand and source vegan alternatives, including handy ingredients to have in your pantry or spice rack to help you whip up something tasty at a moment's notice, as well as recipe heroes perfect for punching up flavour with less work.

We've organised the chapters to suit different times of the day, cravings and occasions:

BRUNCH has dishes to wow at the start of the day, with quick weekday breakfasts and impressive weekend spreads. But it's not just for the morning – lots of these dishes can be adapted for lunch, dinner or even dessert.

SHARING includes smaller plates that can form part of a party spread, but which are equally delicious on their own as a starter or snack. Colour is key with these recipes, making them wow-factor dishes with no fuss.

LIGHT includes dishes to make after a long day when you just need something quick and satisfying. These are our go-to dishes at home when time is short and we need a reliable, delicious meal in minutes.

COMFORT offers plant-based alternatives to some favourite family or occasion meals, such as mac and cheese (see page 97) or sausage and mash (see page 114). This is a great chapter to turn to if you are planning a cosy lunch or dinner for loved ones.

CROWD-PLEASERS is a really fun chapter, with sandwiches, burgers, wraps, enchiladas and more. Many of these meals are interactive, with lots of building, adding and eating with your hands – ideal food to enjoy with friends.

SIDES is full of recipes for those times when you have a few more people to serve or a little more time to prepare. We've selected a range of accompaniments that are versatile and flavour-enhancing.

DRESSINGS & PICKLES contains a broad range of vegan adaptations of classics such as mayonnaise or ranch dressing, plus exciting, flavour-packed sauces and dips. Our pickles are some of our most-requested recipes (especially the Pineapple Achar on page 180!), and we can't wait to share them with you.

SWEET is a chapter of fantastically easy desserts and treats. Dessert can often be the most daunting part of a meal to make yourself, especially when it comes to vegan dessert, but these recipes will give you great results with minimal ingredients, time or work involved. There are even some treats that you can give as gifts for that personal touch.

BAKES will show you how to make classic cakes and cookies that no one will guess are vegan.

Last but not least, **DRINKS** includes some much-loved drinks recipes from our bars. Packed with fruit and fragrance, we have cocktails for everyone, including alcohol-free options.

On most pages, we've also included tips to help you ensure success, adapt recipes or cut a few corners with no compromise on flavour. We want you to make these dishes your own and hope they become firm favourites in your homes, just as they have in ours.

Toolkit

You don't need a load of fancy equipment to make great food and drinks at home, but there are a few items that will make things quicker and easier. Here are our chefs' suggestions for useful tools to have in your kitchen to save you time and ensure great results.

ESSENTIALS

Box grater

A rectangular metal box grater with four size options is almost always going to be better than a fancy one that costs 20 times as much. Also, graters don't stay sharp forever, so it's better to buy one you don't mind replacing at some point.

Knives

You don't need hundreds of expensive knives. For efficient vegetable preparation, we recommend investing in three decent knives: a good bread knife, a small paring knife and a good chopping knife. For chopping, a Japanese-style knife, or *usuba*, is an excellent choice. Its large blade is great for preparing produce of all shapes and sizes, and also for scooping up chopped vegetables to transfer them to the pan.

Knife sharpener

Knives don't have to be new or expensive, but they do have to be sharp. Sharp knives are often safer to use as they slip less and allow you more control and speed as you work. Chefs often use a steel or whetstone to sharpen knives. The technique for both takes some training and skill, but can be learned with practice. Alternatively, you can buy domestic knife-sharpening tools that are simple to use. Some handheld domestic knife sharpeners will wear down your blades and make them uneven, so look for a benchtop one that imitates a steel and doesn't remove too much of the blade.

Pestle and mortar

Such a useful thing to have in the kitchen for grinding roast spices. When you loosely grind spices, you get much more crunch and flavour. An electrical spice grinder is only worth investing in if you are making large amounts of spice mixes at home. There is also really no substitute flavour-wise for making pesto in a pestle and mortar; the flavours released via this method are far superior to making it in a food processor (although both will give better results than most store-bought pestos!). This is why we've given instructions for making pesto both ways in our recipe on page 177.

Stone is the best material for pestle and mortars if you want to make spice pastes and pesto, as it is non-porous and will not absorb flavours and oils. You can find inexpensive wooden pestle and mortars easily; these are great for grinding spices.

Speed or French peeler

This style of peeler is the only kind you will find in our kitchens. It has a wide top and a blade that moves as you peel. It is far quicker to use than other peelers, and great for making ribbon shapes for garnishes.

Stick blender with attachments

If you only buy one electric gadget for your kitchen, this is the one. Whether you're making vegan mayo, blending soup, or whipping up dressings and purées, a stick blender is ideal. If you get the type with a number of different attachments, the little drum attachment makes spice pastes and pesto in seconds, while the whisk attachment is really useful for desserts.

Wok

There is no need to buy a fancy one, but if you want to make a good stir-fry, a wok is essential. We use the simplest woks in medium size; the main consideration is your wok is light enough for you to comfortably move and shake so that you can toss your stir-fries as they cook. Wok-cooking is super fast, and the shape of the wok and speed of cooking means it requires less oil than conventional frying. Quick and healthy, wok cooking is a win-win.

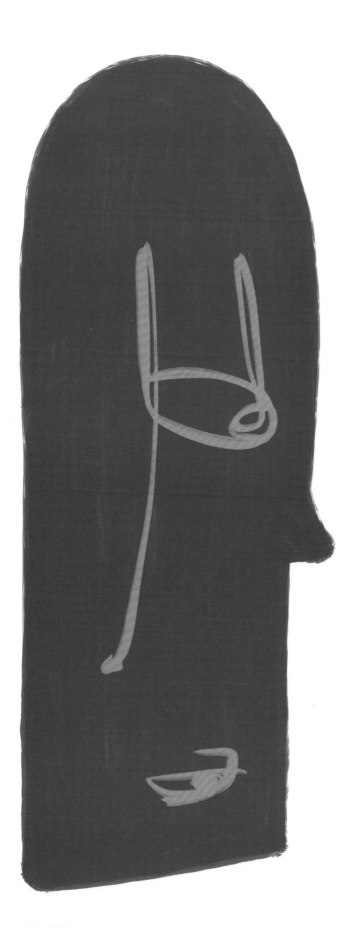

Non-stick frying pan

Non-stick frying pans generally mean you can use less oil. The results are also more consistent.

Sauté pan

A sauté pan is a deep, heavy frying pan. Choose one with an ovenproof handle, designed for cooking either on the stove or in the oven. These pans are so useful, as you can start something off on the hob and then pop it in the oven.

Baking tins and sheets

We use three different baking items:

- a 20cm (8in) cake tin – preferably springform, as they are easier to open without damaging the cake;

- a 23cm (9in) loaf tin – preferably non-stick, as it's easier to remove the finished goods;

- baking sheets.

Shopping guide

If you are new to cooking vegan food, you can feel a bit lost navigating the shops, so we want to give you a guide to finding great vegan ingredients and sourcing alternatives to non-vegan ones. The good news is that shopping vegan has never been easier, with more choices available all the time and more mainstream shops stocking them. It has also become easier to order more specialist items online – so get ready for whole new world of options.

You don't need to buy everything that is listed here. This is a supplementary guide to help you understand how key ingredients work, and how they can or cannot be used in recipes.

OIL

In most recipes, we've suggested using a light oil for cooking – something without a very dominant flavour, such as a light rapeseed, sunflower or olive oil. If we mention a specific oil, like extra virgin olive oil, toasted sesame or cold-pressed rapeseed, it's because we feel that specific flavour will work best for that recipe.

FREEZER

Asian specialist shops usually have loads of great frozen vegan options for dumplings and gyoza. Shops that specialise in South Asian or Indian ingredients are great for stocking up the freezer with breads such as paratha and roti. We also recommend you buy fresh curry leaves and lime leaves and store them in the freezer, as then you can get that amazing fresh herb flavour whenever you need it.

You can also keep a bag of vegetable trimmings – such as onion ends, leek tops and carrot peel – in the freezer for making stock. When you have enough, you can make a big batch of homemade stock and freeze it in small half-litre (18fl oz) bags to use for soups.

DAIRY ALTERNATIVES

The world of plant-based dairy alternatives is ever expanding. Here is how to navigate it.

Vegan butter has recently become widely available. As the name suggests, this is to use in place of butter, and it has a similar fat and water content. This is key for baking. When making a cake, you can sometimes substitute baking margarine (which is mostly vegan, but do check) in place of vegan butter but the flavour is usually not as good. Baking margarine will come in a block; the spreadable margarine in tubs contain lots of liquid and will not work in place of butter.

There is now a very broad range of plant-based milks available. In some recipes, we recommend you use soy milk, and this is because some plant milks do not have enough protein to emulsify, which is important in recipes like mayonnaise. You can use other higher-protein milks in its place, but the results may not be as consistent.

Vegan creams are getting better all the time. For cooking, we use a lentil-based one that is labelled as a 'double cream' and can be found in the fridge aisle of most supermarkets, but we use other kinds as well, including soy- and oat-based creams. Just make sure it is labelled 'double'. The new plant-based double creams whip well but won't hold their shape for as long as regular cream. Also, while most plant-based creams available no longer split when heated, they won't thicken like regular cream.

When it comes to vegan yogurt, we almost always use coconut. It has the shortest ingredients list; a good-quality one should just be coconut milk, vegan biocultures and maybe a little tapioca. It acts just like good, thick regular yogurt in recipes, and has a nice, clean, tangy flavour.

Vegan cheeses are usually made with either nuts or coconut oil. We usually use coconut-based vegan cream cheeses and feta alternatives, but the recipes in this book should work with the nut-based ones too. Nuts absorb more liquid, though, so if you use nut-based cheeses, you may need to increase the liquid in the recipe.

MEAT ALTERNATIVES

Meat alternatives, like chick'n and no-beef burgers, divide people – some hate them, and that's totally fine. For others, they are a great way to reduce or remove the meat in their diet – and if you're doing that, then we think you are doing a good thing. But if meat alternatives aren't for you, don't worry – we've suggested other options in the recipes that use them.

There are so many meat alternative products available now, but there are a couple of things to bear in mind. Most are already seasoned, so check the amount of salt you're using in a dish. Also, many are already cooked and just need to be reheated, but check the cooking times, as they vary quite a bit.

PLANT PROTEINS

We want to talk to you about tofu and tempeh. People can be put off by tofu, but don't make up your mind that you don't like it if you don't understand how diverse it is. It comes in so many forms and is packed full of protein. It tends to only really taste like what you seasoned or cooked it with, so don't blame the tofu – blame the cook!

Silken tofu often comes in packs that can be stored in the pantry. As the name suggests, it is smooth and useful for providing a lovely, silky texture.

Firm tofu is usually found in the fridge aisle, and is often stored in water. A good-quality organic firm tofu holds its texture, but shouldn't be crumbly. It must be drained very well and dried out. If you intend to fry it, it is best to press the liquid out by gently applying even pressure or using a tofu press.

Tofu puffs are squeezed, fried tofu that has puffed up, meaning it will soak up flavours. These are found in the freezer section of most Asian supermarkets.

Tempeh is another soy product, but here the soy beans are left whole and fermented, leaving them with a distinctive nutty texture and taste. It is very diverse in its uses, as it can be fried in strips or cubes, or grated for a fantastic mince texture.

FLAVOUR HEROES

Good-quality **dried mushrooms**, such as dried shiitake and porcini, are a great way to provide intense flavours, as the drying process intensifies the taste.

Chilli oil is so useful for boosting flavours. Be careful, as some contain dried shrimp. We like the type with crispy chilli or black beans. Good-quality chilli pastes such as harissa are also useful for punching up dips and sauces, and are great for tossing through roasted vegetables. Another option is smoky Mexican chipotle chilli paste; it's so easy to use and adds a boost to Mexican dishes.

Miso pastes are a must for adding depth of flavour. You can add them to almost anything to round out the flavour, and they're also packed with protein. We also use gochujang, a Korean chilli paste, quite a lot. Look for a great-quality one with miso, seaweed and *gochugaru* (bright red Korean chilli flakes).

South Asian and Indian **snack mixes**, such as sev, boondi or fried crispy onions, make great toppings to add flavour and texture to dishes. *Furikake*, or Japanese rice seasonings, come in many varieties including chilli, nori and shiso, and are a great way to add flavour to rice, noodles and salads.

If you're not into making your own stock, then **vegan stock cubes** or **powder** are a must. It's nice to have a variety. You can find mushroom, tomato and onion stocks, as well as different-flavoured vegetable stock cubes that can match the flavour of particular recipes better than generic stocks.

FABULOUS FERMENTS

We love ferments, and we have included a few recipes for quickly making your own. However, there are so many great ones available to buy. Hamisha **pickled cucumbers** and thin, vinegary Turkish-style pickled cucumbers make a great addition to sandwiches and toasts. Lebanese-style mixed pickles are fun and add colour. A jar of **pickled beetroot** is a handy and nutritious flavour booster for salads and dips.

We also recommend having jars of **vegan kimchi** available for adding to soups, sandwiches, toasties and stir-fries.

Get to know South Asian or Indian pickles and chutneys; these are packed with flavour. Oil-based Indian pickles or *achar* are made with unique masalas or spice mixes that are tempered into the oil and infuse the pickles with diverse flavours and heat levels. They add game-changing amounts of flavour. They aren't just condiments; they can be added to sauces and used as marinades. We love *brinjal* (aubergine) and hot mango.

SPICE RACK

What's the difference between whole and ground spices? Whole spices can be toasted and slightly crushed, which means they work really well in recipes where they can release flavour slowly without burning or becoming bitter. They add little pops of flavour that brighten up dishes. Ground spices need little or no cooking, and release flavour more evenly.

Our ideal desert-island spice rack would include the following:

coriander seeds

ground coriander

ground cinnamon

whole nutmeg

ground nutmeg

cumin seeds

ground cumin

mild pul biber (Aleppo pepper)

Korean *gochugaru* chilli flakes

ground turmeric

black and pink peppercorns

mustard seeds

whole cardamom

whole star anise

ground allspice

We also refer to some dried Mexican chillies in the recipes. These are available from delis and wholefood shops, or anywhere that specialises in Mexican or Latin American products. They are also readily available to order online.

A NOTE ON SALT

When we simply say 'salt' in this book, we are referring to good-quality granulated sea salt. We also refer to sea salt flakes, which add texture and crunch. The other important salt you'll find here is *kala namak* or black salt. Black salt is kiln-fired sulphurised salt, and is a very commonly used ingredient in South Asia and India. It has a very strong, eggy taste, so acts as the base flavour in a lot of egg-replacement recipes. You will see it used in most *chaat* or snack mixes too. The sulphur smell can be intense, so you may want to open a window after using it.

ACCIDENTALLY VEGAN

First things first, check the labels. Yes, there are a few frustrating times when manufacturers sneak milk or egg into things that shouldn't really need them, but you will also be amazed how many mainstream items just happen to be vegan, especially things like breads, snacks, biscuits, and most decent dark chocolate and chocolate chips. Sometimes recipes change, however, so if it's not advertised as vegan, you should check the label every time you buy, just in case.

One thing that is usually vegan and is a great time-saving product is shop-bought fresh pastry, like puff, shortcrust and filo. Check the packet, but most mainstream brands are dairy- and egg-free.

A word of warning, though: there is currently no legal definition of vegan, and vegan doesn't mean allergen-free. Please be aware that items labelled as vegan can still have traces of milk and egg. If you are cooking for guests with allergies, then be extra vigilant and look for 'free-from' labelled items.

Pantry

A well-stocked pantry makes great cooking easier. Good-quality canned, chopped or crushed **tomatoes** and bottles of passata are worth the extra cost (we like the Mutti brand). We also think you'll come to love canned **jackfruit** as a quick meal hero, because it's so quick to cook and takes on flavour brilliantly. Canned **coconut milk** is always useful. When you buy canned or jarred **beans** and **pulses**, buy the best you can afford. They are still relatively cheap and are a great source of protein.

Dried **lentils** are also a great thing to have on hand. When it comes to quick cooking, red lentils and urad dal are the fastest. We recommend buying pulses from local shops that specialise in Indian ingredients, as they tend to be a fraction of the price of little supermarket packets. Always wash dried pulses well before cooking.

A selection of quick-cook **noodles** like soba, rice or mung vermicelli and udon are useful. I usually have both basmati and long-grain **rice**, as they are useful for different things: basmati for flavour and long-grain as it stays softer for longer. The cooking times given in this book are for white rice; be aware that brown rice has a much longer cooking time. For any wholegrain rice, we recommend washing and soaking overnight, as this will make the cooking time shorter and stop the grains from splitting.

Keep a few special **flours** for thickening and frying. In this book, you will see rice flour, tapioca and cornflour. These are useful for replacing egg in dishes, providing texture to sauces and creating a crisp coating for frying. Asian specialist shops are a good place to buy these. You will also find good-quality panko breadcrumbs, which are great for crumbing and coating.

In terms of sweets, vegan chocolate-and-hazelnut spread and other **sweet spreads** (we like Lotus Biscoff) are useful for quick desserts. Bars of **dark chocolate** or chocolate chips are also very handy.

You will also see reference to **vegan gelling agents** in some of the dessert recipes. These are vegan gelatine substitutes, and are much easier to use than gelatine. They come in little packets in the baking area of the supermarket and can also be purchased online.

brunch

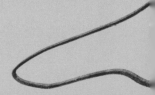

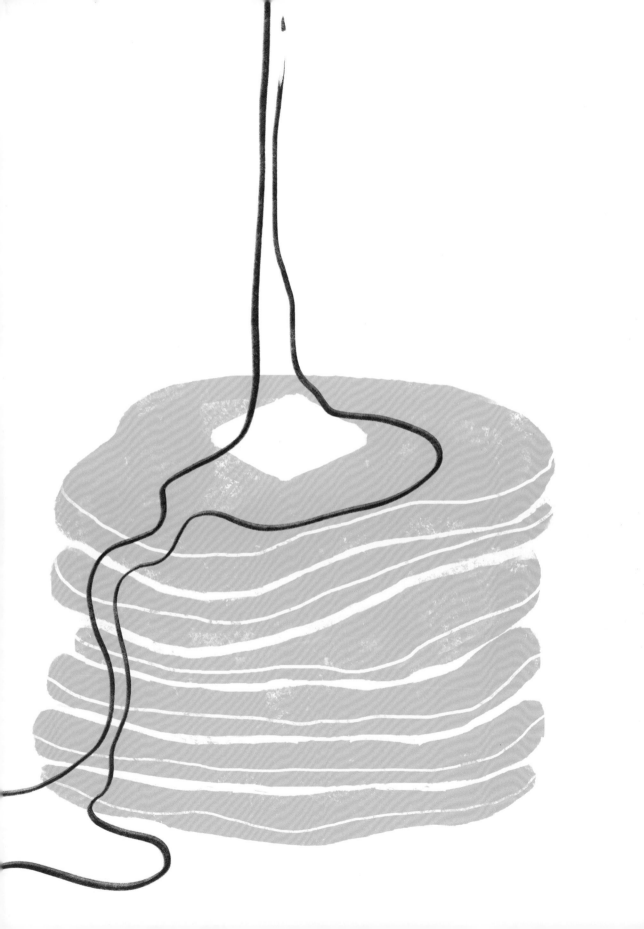

CHERRY PISTACHIO PORRIDGE

We call this 'executive porridge' because this is not your bog-standard daily breakfast; this is a warm, cosy bowl of luxury. We use organic gluten-free porridge oats, but you can use any porridge oats you like.

SERVES 1–2

50G (1¾OZ) PORRIDGE OATS

150ML (¼ PINT) WATER

200ML (7FL OZ) PLANT-BASED CREAM

PINCH OF SALT

1 TABLESPOON SOFT LIGHT BROWN SUGAR OR 2 TABLESPOONS MAPLE/AGAVE SYRUP

To serve

2–4 TABLESPOONS BLACK CHERRY COMPOTE (see page 204, or use shop-bought)

½ TABLESPOON PISTACHIOS, chopped or sliced

GROUND CINNAMON, for dusting

CHEF'S TIP

If you need to reheat, add a little more liquid.

1) Combine the oats, water, cream, salt and sugar or syrup in a small pan over a medium heat.

2) Bring the mixture to a gentle simmer, then cook for 5 minutes, whisking constantly, until the oats are broken down and the mixture has reached your desired consistency (add more water if necessary).

3) Drizzle over the cherry compote and scatter over the pistachios, then finish with a light dusting of cinnamon and serve.

PEANUT BUTTER & JAM OVERNIGHT OATS

If you're the kind of person who aspires to eat a healthy, filling breakfast but also likes pressing the snooze button, these overnight oats are for you. You can prepare the pots the night before and they'll be ready to eat in the morning, even if you need to eat on the run. You can mix up the flavours – and don't worry if you're not a peanut fan, as this recipe still works without the nut butter.

1) In a bowl, mix the peanut butter with a splash of the almond milk to loosen, then add the remaining almond milk along with the oats, chia seeds, yogurt and jam.

2) Mix everything together well with a spatula, then scoop into 2 jam jars or bowls. Cover and refrigerate overnight.

3) The next morning, stir well and add another splash of almond milk if the mixture looks too firm. Top with a little more jam, the sliced apples and fresh berries and a sprinkle of chopped peanuts, and serve.

MAKES 2 POTS

1½ TABLESPOONS PEANUT BUTTER (crunchy or smooth – your choice)

300ML (½ PINT) UNSWEETENED ALMOND MILK, or any plant-based milk, plus extra to serve if needed

150G (5½OZ) ROLLED OATS

2 TABLESPOONS CHIA SEEDS

1 TABLESPOON PLAIN PLANT-BASED YOGURT

1½ TABLESPOONS RASPBERRY JAM (blackcurrant or strawberry also work well), plus a little extra to serve

To serve

1 APPLE, sliced

A HANDFUL OF FRESH BERRIES

2 TEASPOONS CHOPPED SALTED PEANUTS

BUTTERMILK PANCAKES WITH TROPICAL FRUIT SALAD

Delivering all the fluff you will ever need, our buttermilk pancakes are undisputed brunch champions. We are so happy that coconut yogurt made with coconut milk and natural vegan live cultures is now readily available. It means that when you add it to plant milk, you can make a vegan buttermilk that really gives these pancakes a mega lift.

The pancake batter will look like it's far too thick, but it needs to be much thicker than conventional pancake batter. And there's no need to believe the old story that the first pancake is always rubbish! Usually the reason the first one ends up in the bin is that your pan is either too hot or too cold, meaning you get either a burned pancake or a stodgy mess. It can also be because you have used too much butter or oil, making it too greasy. Just prepare the pan well and you should be good to go.

MAKES 6–8

350ML (12FL OZ) SOY OR ALMOND MILK

1½ TABLESPOONS RAPESEED OIL

2 TABLESPOONS MAPLE SYRUP

½ TABLESPOON COCONUT YOGURT

½ TEASPOON LEMON JUICE

250G (9OZ) SELF-RAISING FLOUR

2 TEASPOONS BAKING POWDER

25G (1OZ) CASTER SUGAR

PINCH OF SALT

PINCH OF GROUND CINNAMON OR NUTMEG (optional)

PLANT-BASED BUTTER OR RAPESEED OIL, for frying

For the fruit salad

100ML (3½FL OZ) PASSION FRUIT COULIS (if you can't find this, use 50ml/2fl oz tropical fruit juice)

2 KIWI FRUIT, peeled and sliced

1 RIPE MANGO, peeled and cubed

2 BANANAS, sliced

To serve

100G (3½OZ) COCONUT YOGURT

MAPLE OR AGAVE SYRUP, to taste

1) Combine the milk, oil, syrup, yogurt and lemon juice in a jug, stirring to form a smooth buttermilk. Set aside.

2) In a large bowl, sift together the flour and baking powder, then add the sugar, salt and cinnamon or nutmeg (if using).

3) Make a well in the centre of the dry mixture and gradually pour in the vegan buttermilk in stages, whisking well between each addition to incorporate. Once combined, leave the batter to sit for at least 15 minutes (you can make the mixture up to 4 hours in advance if you want to).

4) Meanwhile, make the fruit salad by combining all the ingredients in a bowl and mixing well.

5) To cook the pancakes, place a large non-stick frying pan over a medium heat. Leave the pan on the heat for at least 3 minutes to get nice and hot, then add a little butter or rapeseed oil to the pan and, using a heatproof brush or kitchen paper, smear the butter or oil evenly across the pan.

6) Reduce the heat to low and, using a very large serving spoon or a ladle, put a tidy scoop of the batter into the pan (you want 80–100g/2¾–3½oz of mixture per scoop). Don't spread it out, as it will spread naturally. Add as many scoops as will fit in the pan (usually 2–3).

7) When you see bubbles appearing on the surface of the pancakes, carefully turn with a clean spatula to cook on the other side. You're waiting for all the raising agent and flour to cook out, which will take about 2½ minutes on each side. The cooked pancakes should be golden and well risen, and should feel light and hollow when you lift them.

8) Transfer the cooked pancakes to a warm plate covered with a clean cloth to keep warm while you cook the remainder, brushing more oil or butter across the pan if needed.

9) To serve, divide the pancakes between serving plates and serve topped with the fruit salad, along with a dollop of coconut yogurt and a good drizzle of maple or agave syrup.

CHOCOLATE HAZELNUT CRÊPES

Crêpes are the sexiest pancake, in our opinion. Thin and not too filling, their delicate texture is perfect for rich toppings, making them just as good for dessert as they are for breakfast. If you don't have hazelnut spread, you can simply grate chocolate and sprinkle it over the warm crêpes so it melts inside.

MAKES 8

450G (1LB) PLAIN FLOUR

2 TEASPOONS CORNFLOUR

8 TEASPOONS CASTER SUGAR

PINCH OF SALT

800ML (27FL OZ) PLANT-BASED MILK

60G (2¼OZ) PLANT-BASED BUTTER, melted

PLANT-BASED BUTTER OR VEGETABLE OIL, for frying

To serve

8 TABLESPOONS VEGAN HAZELNUT CHOCOLATE SPREAD

8 STRAWBERRIES, hulled and sliced

ICING SUGAR, for dusting

CHEF'S TIP

A 125g (4½oz) scoop of the batter will perfectly cover the base of a pan measuring 28cm (11in) in diameter.

To make a savoury crêpe, simply omit the sugar from the recipe and fill the crêpe with spinach and mushrooms, your favourite vegan cheese or another savoury filling of your choice.

1) In a large bowl, mix together the plain flour, cornflour, sugar and salt. In a jug, mix together the plant-based milk and melted butter.

2) Make a well in the centre of the flour mixture. Pour the milk and the butter mixture into the well in stages, whisking vigorously between each addition to form a smooth batter. The batter should be slightly thick, but still runnier than a conventional pancake batter. If you lift the whisk, you should be able to draw the number 8 with the batter in the bowl.

3) Place a large non-stick frying pan or crêpe pan over a medium heat. Leave it on the heat for at least 3 minutes to warm, then add a little plant-based butter or vegetable oil to the pan and, using a heatproof brush or kitchen paper, smear the butter or oil evenly across the pan.

4) Using a ladle, place a scoop of the batter into the pan (see Chef's Tip), then tip and rotate the pan to spread the batter out as thinly as possible.

5) Cook for 2 minutes, or until you see bubbles forming in the centre of the crêpe. This means it's time to flip. If you like, you can simply do this using a clean spatula, but if you're feeling confident and want to flip like a pro, gently shake the pan to loosen the side of the crêpe, then slide the crêpe to the edge of the pan and flip, catching it flat on the other side.

6) Cook the crêpe for 1 minute on the other side, then transfer to a warm plate covered with a clean cloth to keep warm while you cook the remainder.

7) To serve, spread one half of each crêpe with 1 tablespoon vegan hazelnut chocolate spread and arrange a sliced strawberry on top. Fold the crêpe in half then in half again, then dust with icing sugar. Enjoy!

RED PEPPER ONE-PAN SCRAMBLED TOFU

Scrambled tofu is a key part of our breakfast menu, and we have tweaked and updated the recipe over the years. The vegetables add lots of extra colour and flavour. The tofu mixture can be prepped the night before and stored in a sealed container in the fridge, ready to use in the morning; in fact, this way, it tastes even better. Just don't add the plant-based cream and vegetables until the next day.

SERVES 2–4

250G (9OZ) FIRM TOFU, drained

¼ TEASPOON GROUND TURMERIC

1 TEASPOON *KALA NAMAK* (black salt)

⅛ TEASPOON GROUND BLACK PEPPER

1 TABLESPOON NUTRITIONAL YEAST

3–4 TABLESPOONS LIGHT OIL, such as rapeseed or vegetable oil

3 GARLIC CLOVES, grated or finely chopped

½ SMALL ONION, diced

1 SMALL RED PEPPER, diced

100ML (3½FL OZ) PLANT-BASED CREAM

2 SPRING ONIONS, trimmed and sliced

1) Combine the tofu, turmeric, black salt, pepper and nutritional yeast in a bowl and mash together. Be prepared for the strong eggy smell of the black salt! Set aside.

2) Heat the oil in a frying pan over a medium heat. Add the garlic and onion and cook for 2 minutes until translucent, then add the red pepper and cook through for 3 minutes or so. Now add the tofu mixture and fry, stirring, for 4–5 minutes.

3) Just before serving, add the cream to achieve a scrambled egg consistency. Finally, scatter over the spring onions and serve.

BAGELS & SCHMEARS

Our schmears will take your bagels to the next level. We've gone for a good mix of textures and colours; they are all great individually, but when combined make an impressive brunch spread. They can all be prepared in advance, so you can show off your skills without the drama of a last-minute scramble in the kitchen.

HERB & PICKLE CREAM CHEESE

We are a pickled cucumber family, and my daughter will happily finish a jar of pickles, juice and all, if left to her own devices. I prefer Haimisha pickles, but use any type of pickled cucumber you enjoy: sweet, vinegary, salty or even cornichons.

SERVES 2–3, or more as part of a spread

150G (5½OZ) PLANT-BASED CREAM CHEESE

ZEST OF ½ LEMON, finely grated

1 TABLESPOON CHIVES, very finely chopped

1 TABLESPOON DILL, finely chopped, plus extra sprigs to garnish

1 GARLIC CLOVE, finely grated

3 TABLESPOONS DILL PICKLES (ABOUT 30G/1OZ), finely diced

SALT AND FRESHLY GROUND BLACK PEPPER

CARROT RIBBONS, to garnish (optional – see Chef's Tip)

1) In a bowl, use a fork or spoon to stir the cream cheese a little to loosen it up. Add the other ingredients (except the carrot ribbons) and combine well.

2) Season the cream cheese mixture to taste, then smear generously on lightly toasted bagels or bread. Garnish with dill sprigs and, if you want to dress it up a little, carrot ribbons.

CHEF'S TIP

To make carrot ribbons, use a peeler to remove the skin of a carrot and discard, then continue to peel the carrot into long ribbons. Put these in iced water for a few minutes, and they will start to curl up. Drain and use as a garnish.

CONTINUED ON PAGE 28...

SEE IMAGE, OVERLEAF

mushroom parfait →

v'egg mayo

beetroot &
dill cream cheese

herb & pickle
cream cheese

MUSHROOM PARFAIT

This parfait is super smooth and packed with flavour. Make it a few hours in advance of serving to allow it time to cool.

SERVES 2–3, or more as part of a spread

2 TABLESPOONS VEGETABLE OR RAPESEED OIL

3 GARLIC CLOVES, finely sliced

2 TABLESPOONS OREGANO LEAVES, chopped

300G (10½OZ) CHESTNUT MUSHROOMS, sliced

½ TEASPOON SALT

¼ TEASPOON FRESHLY GROUND BLACK PEPPER

150ML (¼ PINT) PLANT-BASED CREAM

WATERCRESS, to garnish

1) Heat the oil in a non-stick frying pan over a medium heat. Add the garlic and cook gently for a couple of minutes to infuse.

2) Increase the heat to medium–high, then add the oregano and mushrooms. Cook for 5 minutes, stirring from time to time, until the mushrooms are cooked through and turning slightly golden on the edges. Take care not to burn the garlic.

3) Season with the salt and pepper. Set a few mushrooms aside for the garnish, then add the cream to the pan and cook for 2 minutes more.

4) Scoop the mushroom mixture into a high-powered blender and blend until completely smooth.

5) Using a spatula, scoop the parfait into a bowl or serving dish and smooth the top. Chill completely before serving with toasted bagels, garnished with the reserved mushrooms and watercress.

CHEF'S TIP

A small splash of Port can be added along with the mushrooms to elevate this schmear.

BEETROOT & DILL CREAM CHEESE

The beetroot gives this schmear a lovely vibrant colour and sweet finish. Pickled beetroot works really well for this recipe, but if you can't find it, just use cooked beetroot and add 1 teaspoon cider or red wine vinegar. This is fantastic on toasted rye bread as well as bagels.

SERVES 2–3, or more as part of a spread

150G PLANT-BASED CREAM CHEESE

100G PICKLED BEETROOT, grated (use the big holes on your grater), plus extra slices to garnish

¼ TEASPOON CARAWAY SEEDS, crushed with a pestle and mortar

1 TABLESPOON DILL, chopped, plus extra sprigs to garnish

SALT AND FRESHLY GROUND BLACK PEPPER

To garnish (optional)

SLICED RED ONION RINGS

A HANDFUL OF CAPERS

1) In a bowl, use a whisk to whip the cream cheese a little to loosen. Add the other ingredients and combine well.

2) Season to taste, then smear generously on lightly toasted bagels or bread. Garnish with some sliced pickled beetroot, dill sprigs, sliced red onion rings and a scattering of capers, if you like.

SWEETCORN FRITTERS

The bright colour of these fritters will really bring the sunshine in. They are a great gluten-free breakfast option, but also work well as a starter or as part of a party spread. If you like a bit of heat, feel free to punch up the quantity of chilli a bit. We've included a recipe for a cooling homemade vegan sour cream as well, as this pairs brilliantly with the hot fritters straight out of the pan.

1) To make the vegan sour cream, combine all the ingredients in a bowl and set aside.

2) For the fritters, place half the sweetcorn in a large bowl. Add the lime juice and mash with a stick blender to combine and break apart the corn. If you don't have a stick blender, finely chop the sweetcorn, then mash it together with the lime juice using a whisk.

3) Add the remaining corn, along with the cornflour, flour, salt and diced vegetables. Mix well, then add the sparkling water and stir to combine.

4) Pour oil into a large non-stick frying pan to a depth of 2–3mm ($^1/_{16}$–$^1/_8$in) and place over a medium heat. Heat the oil to 180°C (350°F). If you don't have a cooking thermometer, you can test to see if the oil is ready by dropping in a little of the mixture. It should bubble around the batter, but not spit.

5) Working in batches, use a serving spoon to drop 50g (1¾oz) spoonfuls of the mixture carefully into the oil, gently pressing down with the back of the spoon to make a 1cm (½in) thick patty. Don't overcrowd the pan. Adjust the heat if needed; you want to cook these quite gently, so that small bubbles are forming around the fritters, but they're not spitting. Cook for about 3 minutes until golden, then carefully flip the fritters and cook for another 3 minutes on the other side. Once cooked, transfer to a plate in a low oven, and repeat with the remaining mixture.

6) Serve hot with the sour cream and any of the suggested trimmings that take your fancy.

MAKES 8

180G (6½OZ) SWEETCORN (if using frozen, defrost; if using canned, drain well)

JUICE OF ½ LIME

20G (¾OZ) CORNFLOUR

110G (3¾OZ) GLUTEN-FREE SELF-RAISING FLOUR

½ TEASPOON SALT

½ SMALL RED CHILLI, diced

½ SMALL ONION, diced

½ SMALL RED PEPPER, very finely diced

1 SPRING ONION, finely sliced

100ML (3½FL OZ) SPARKLING WATER

LIGHT OIL, such as rapeseed or vegetable oil, for frying

For the vegan sour cream

100G (3½OZ) COCONUT YOGURT

75ML (5 TABLESPOONS) PLANT-BASED CREAM

ZEST AND JUICE OF ½ LIME

SALT, to taste

To serve (optional)

SALAD LEAVES

QUICK PICO DE GALLO (see page 135)

JALAPEÑOS, sliced

FRESH CORIANDER, chopped

TWO-TOFU SANDO

Sando is the Japanese name for the sandwich, and the flavours of *sando* in Japan are as diverse as they are elsewhere in the world. They are usually beautifully presented on white bread with the crusts scrupulously removed and the *sando* carefully cut in half to reveal the delicious filling inside. One of the most popular types is an egg *sando* with two types of egg – hard-boiled and egg mayo – so we've recreated that here with our two-tofu version, featuring v'egg mayo and a bacon-glazed fried tofu. It's bonkers how well it works.

The bacon glaze is a great recipe, as it makes such a useful marinade (we also use it in our Smoky Chickpea Cobb Salad on page 85). It keeps well in a clean jar for at least a week.

1) For the bacon glaze, measure all the ingredients into a clean jar. Put on the lid and vigorously shake to combine. Alternatively, whisk together in a bowl.

2) Pour the glaze into a shallow bowl, and tip the cornflour on to a plate or into a shallow bowl. Take a tofu slice and dip it into the glaze, then into the cornflour, then again into the glaze and set aside on a clean plate while you repeat with the remaining slices.

3) Heat a splash of sesame oil in a large non-stick frying pan over a medium heat. Add the tofu slices and cook for a couple of minutes on each side until slightly crispy.

4) To prepare the sandwiches, carefully trim off the crusts of the bread, then spread aioli on 2 of the slices and the v'egg mayo on the other slices. Divide the tofu between the 2 aioli slices, then carefully top with the v'egg mayo slices, but don't squish down.

5) Using a long, sharp knife or bread knife, cut through the centre of the first *sando*. Clean the knife before cutting the next *sando*.

6) Place the 2 halves of each sandwich on top of each other and serve. If you like, you can dress it up with a garnish of cucumber ribbons.

SERVES 2

40G (1½OZ) CORNFLOUR

260G (9¼OZ) FIRM TOFU, drained well and sliced into 1.5cm (⅝in) slices

SESAME OIL, for frying

4 THICK SLICES OF WHITE SANDWICH BREAD

2 TABLESPOONS VEGAN AIOLI (see page 170 to make your own)

4 TABLESPOONS V'EGG MAYO (see page 36)

CUCUMBER RIBBONS, to garnish (optional)

For the bacon glaze

2 TABLESPOONS TOMATO PURÉE

½ TEASPOON SMOKED PAPRIKA

½ TEASPOON NUTRITIONAL YEAST

½ TEASPOON GARLIC POWDER

100ML (3½FL OZ) SOY SAUCE OR TAMARI

100G (3½OZ) SOFT LIGHT BROWN SUGAR

1 TABLESPOON MAPLE SYRUP

2 TABLESPOONS LIQUID SMOKE

4 TABLESPOONS VEGETABLE OIL

TURKISH-STYLE BRUNCH

Better known as *kahvalti*, Turkish breakfast is the most important meal of the day. It isn't just about the food; it's considered a social activity, like an early party. I'll never forget the first Turkish breakfast I ever had in Bodrum. I couldn't believe my eyes as the food just kept coming: fresh bread, ripe tomatoes with salt and oil, cucumbers, yogurt, rose jam – it went and on and on, filling the table. It's one of the best examples of eating with all your senses. As a vegan, this type of spread is one of the easiest to convert, as salad dips and perfect seasonal vegetables are the stars of the show. A traditional Turkish breakfast includes a variety of bite-sized delicacies and salads. We've suggested a few, but you don't need to use all of them; choose what you like and improvise. Warm bread is essential, though. The Chickpea *Çılbır*, our version of the classic Turkish egg dish, will give you beautiful centrepiece to build around. We recommend getting the best-quality chickpeas (the type that come in a jar) for this recipe.

SERVES 4

For the chickpea çılbır

100G (3½OZ) PLANT-BASED BUTTER

540G (1LB 3OZ) JAR CHICKPEAS, rinsed and drained

2 TEASPOONS RAS EL HANOUT

200G (7OZ) BABY SPINACH

EXTRA VIRGIN OLIVE OIL AND ALEPPO PEPPER (PUL BIBER), to serve

---

For the spiced yogurt

350G (12OZ) COCONUT YOGURT

1 TEASPOON GROUND CUMIN

1 GARLIC CLOVE, grated

ZEST AND JUICE OF ½ LEMON

½ TEASPOON SALT

1) To make the chickpea çılbır, melt the butter in a frying pan over a medium heat. Add the chickpeas and toss to coat in the butter, then stir in the ras el hanout and cook for a couple of minutes. Add the spinach, then turn off the heat and stir until the leaves have wilted.

2) Meanwhile, make the spiced yogurt by combining all the ingredients in a mixing bowl and bringing together with a whisk.

3) Smear the yogurt on a plate in a circle, then scoop the chickpeas and spinach into the centre of the circle.

4) To finish, drizzle over the olive oil and sprinkle with the pepper flakes, then serve with your chosen brunch elements for a Turkish feast.

To create a spread

MIXED OLIVES

HUMMUS (see page 44)

MIXED CHERRY AND PLUM TOMATOES

QUICK PICKLED CUCUMBER (see page 183)

BEETS & NEEPS PICKLES (see page 166), or shop-bought mixed vegetable pickles

WARM FRESH BREAD

YOUR FAVOURITE JAMS

KIMCHI GRILLED CHEEZE

Grilled cheese is a go-to after-school snack in the States. The trick to ensuring that the cheese is well melted is to pop it in the microwave before frying. The sandwich should be pressed down while frying until the sandwich is golden. Kimchi adds an extra layer of flavour and it pairs really well with toasted sourdough. We use a smoked vegan cheese for ours, which works brilliantly. A perfect light lunch or weekend brunch.

1) To assemble the sandwich, spread half the vegan cheese on to one slice of bread. Top with the kimchi, then sprinkle over the spring onions. Put the rest of the vegan cheese on top and close the sandwich with the second slice of bread.

2) Heat a splash of sesame oil in a small frying pan over a low heat. While it's warming up, pop the sandwich in the microwave for 20–30 seconds, then transfer to the trying pan. Fry lightly, pressing down on the sandwich with something heatproof and flat (a saucepan lid or another, smaller, frying pan work well).

3) Turn the sandwich over and toast on the other side (you may need to add a little more oil).

4) Once the sandwich is cooked to your liking, remove from the pan, cut in half and enjoy. It's delicious as it is, but we like to serve with a bit of Gochujang Sesame Mayo or *furikake*.

SERVES 1

50–60G (1¾–2¼OZ) VEGAN CHEESE, sliced or grated

2 SLICES OF SOURDOUGH BREAD

60–70G (2¼–2½OZ) VEGAN KIMCHI, squeezed well to remove excess liquid

1 SPRING ONION, finely sliced

SESAME OIL, for frying

GOCHUJANG SESAME MAYO (see page 171) or *FURIKAKE* (RICE SEASONING), to serve (optional)

V'EGG MAYO MUFFIN

Rich and satisfying, with the bonus of being absolutely packed with protein, this v'egg mayo is wildly convincing. The mixture of firm and soft tofu makes the texture very eggy. The *kala namak*, or black salt, is doing most of the heavy lifting here, delivering a delicious egg-like flavour. I like to make this with garlic mayo when I have it, but any vegan mayonnaise will work.

SERVES 2–4

4 ENGLISH MUFFINS

PLANT-BASED BUTTER, for spreading

2 TABLESPOONS MUSTARD SPROUTS, to garnish

For the v'egg mayo (see image on page 27)

70G (2½OZ) VEGAN MAYO (shop-bought or see our recipes on page 170)

¼ TEASPOON GROUND TURMERIC

1 TEASPOON *KALA NAMAK* (black salt)

200G (7OZ) FIRM TOFU, drained

100G (3½OZ) SILKEN TOFU, drained

1 TABLESPOON CHIVES, finely sliced

FRESHLY GROUND BLACK PEPPER

1) To make the v'egg mayo, combine the mayonnaise, turmeric and *kala namak* in a small mixing bowl. Season with a few twists of black pepper and mix well with a whisk to combine, making sure there are no lumps.

2) Using your hands, crumble the firm tofu into the bowl, then add the silken tofu, breaking it up just a little – it will naturally break down as you mix. Using a spoon, fold both tofus into the mayonnaise mixture. Work out any big chunks, but don't over-mix.

3) Cut the muffins in half and place under the grill until lightly toasted. Spread with a little plant-based butter.

4) Place 2 tablespoons of the v'egg mayo on top of each muffin half. Season with a little more black pepper, then garnish with the mustard sprouts before serving.

TEMPEH BLT CIABATTA

Tempeh BLT (which I guess should be TBLT) was a go-to chef's breakfast for us before we put it on the menu. The BLT is a masterclass in combining flavours: crunchy bread, rich aioli, crispy lettuce, sweet, ripe tomato, sharp onion and, in this case, rich, smoky tempeh. Tempeh is the perfect vehicle for our bacon glaze, as it soaks up flavour and has a delicious nutty taste when fried. Although it's super tasty, this tempeh won't deliver the crunch of crispy bacon – which is where the ciabatta comes in. With its thin, crunchy shell and soft interior, we think you'll agree it complements the components perfectly.

1) Pour the glaze into a shallow bowl and add the tempeh. Turn to coat and set aside for a few minutes while you prepare the other ingredients.

2) Heat the oil in a non-stick frying pan over a low heat. Add the tempeh slices and fry for 3–4 minutes until caramelised but not burned, then turn and fry on the other side for a further 2 minutes, until browned and slightly crispy.

3) Prepare the ciabatta by slicing it open and lightly toasting it under the grill. Alternatively, warm it through whole in a low oven and then slice it open.

4) Spread the aioli on the top and bottom halves of the ciabatta. Place the tomato slices on the bottom half, followed by the lettuce, then the tempeh, and finally the onion rings.

5) Close the sandwich and cut in half to serve.

SERVES 2

100ML (3½FL OZ) BACON GLAZE (see page 31)

200G (7OZ) TEMPEH, cut into long, thin slices about 5mm (¼in) thick

2 TABLESPOONS VEGETABLE OR RAPESEED OIL

1 CIABATTA (about 300g/ 10½oz)

80G (2¾OZ) VEGAN MAYO OR AIOLI (see page 170)

1 BEEF TOMATO OR 3 PLUM TOMATOES, trimmed, cored and sliced

8 BABY GEM LETTUCE LEAVES, OR 2–3 ROMAINE LETTUCE LEAVES

½ RED ONION, finely sliced and rings separated

Swap it! →

This sandwich is also amazing with sliced avocado, making it a TBLTA – which is a bit of a mouthful, but delicious!

sharing

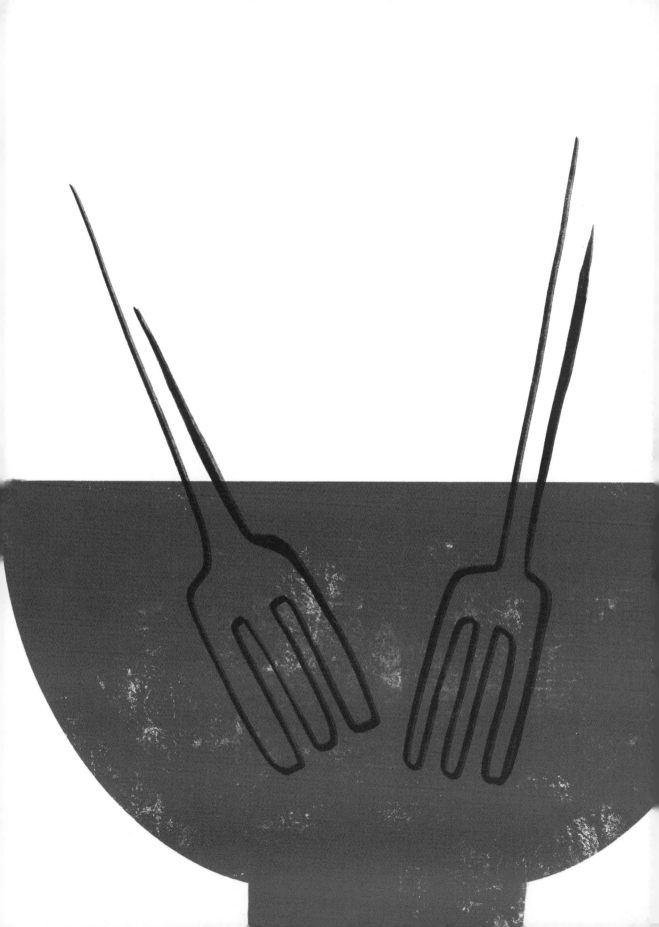

MELON CEVICHE

Ceviche is a Peruvian dish where raw ingredients (in this case, ripe melon slices) are dressed in *leche de tigre* to macerate. *Leche de tigre*, meaning 'tiger's milk', is a citrus-based, spicy marinade. This refreshing, summery recipe uses three types of melon, but you can pick your favourite and use only one – or as many as you like.

SERVES 4–6 as a starter or as part of a spread

150G (5½OZ) CANTALOUPE MELON, finely sliced

150G (5½OZ) HONEYDEW MELON, finely sliced

200G (7OZ) WATERMELON, finely sliced

1 JALAPEÑO, sliced

1 BANANA SHALLOT, sliced and soaked in iced water to remove some of the bite

A FEW MICRO CORIANDER LEAVES

¼ TEASPOON PINK PEPPERCORNS, crushed in a pestle and mortar

For the tiger's milk

150ML (5FL OZ) LIME JUICE (ABOUT 4 LIMES)

1 TABLESPOON CIDER VINEGAR

100ML (3½FL OZ) AGAVE SYRUP

1) To make the tiger's milk, combine all the ingredients in a bowl and stir well until the agave is dissolved.

2) To assemble the salad, arrange the melon slices on a serving dish, overlapping them decoratively.

3) Pour the tiger's milk over the melon and leave to macerate for at least 15 minutes.

4) Garnish with the jalapeño, shallot, coriander leaves and some crushed pink peppercorn and serve immediately.

WALNUT COURGETTE ROLLS

Small, young courgettes are better for these rolls, as they are usually more tender and sweeter. These rolls make a lovely light finger food to serve with drinks and other snacks.

1) To make the courgette pickle, top and tail the courgettes, then slice them lengthways into thin strips, using a French-style vegetable peeler or a mandoline. You will need 12 slices.

2) Prepare the pickle liquid by combining the cider vinegar, water and sugar in a small saucepan over a medium heat. Bring to the boil, then take off the heat and leave to cool.

3) Once cooled, add the courgette slices to the liquid and leave to sit for 2 hours.

4) When you're ready to make the rolls, mix the whipped feta with the basil and chopped walnuts in a bowl.

5) Place 1 teaspoon of the whipped feta mixture on to one end of a courgette strip and roll it up. Repeat until you have used up all the filling.

6) Arrange the rolls upright on a plate. Grind over some black pepper, drizzle with a good-quality extra virgin olive oil, and garnish with the halved grapes, extra walnut pieces and dill sprigs.

MAKES 12

200G (7OZ) WHIPPED FETA (see page 61)

HANDFUL OF BASIL LEAVES, chopped

50G (1¾OZ) TOASTED WALNUTS, chopped, plus extra to garnish

EXTRA VIRGIN OLIVE OIL, for drizzling

FRESHLY GROUND BLACK PEPPER

For the courgette pickle

2 SMALL COURGETTES

100G (3½OZ) CIDER VINEGAR

100ML (3½FL OZ) WATER

60G (2¼OZ) CASTER SUGAR

To garnish

6 BLACK GRAPES, halved

DILL SPRIGS

HUMMUS

The secret to our rich, super-creamy hummus is high-quality ingredients. We have always used very excellent Spanish chickpeas from Brindisa. These are already salted, and so do not require additional seasoning.

For the hummus it isn't necessary to drain the chickpeas completely, as the water they come in (known as aquafaba) is protein rich and makes the hummus even creamier.

SERVES 4 as a starter

250G (9OZ) JARRED CHICKPEAS, lightly drained, plus extra to garnish

35G (1¼OZ) GOOD-QUALITY TAHINI

2 TEASPOONS FRESHLY SQUEEZED LEMON JUICE (about ½ lemon)

1 GARLIC CLOVE, grated

½ TEASPOON GROUND CUMIN, plus extra to garnish

WATER, as needed

EXTRA VIRGIN OLIVE OIL, for drizzling

SALT

1) Combine the chickpeas, tahini, lemon juice, garlic and cumin in a blender or food processor and blend until completely smooth, adding a little water as needed. This will take up to 10 minutes (seriously, the longer the better) depending on how powerful your blender is. Season to taste with salt.

2) Serve straight away, garnished with extra chickpeas, ground cumin and a drizzle of olive oil, or transfer to an airtight container and store in the fridge for up to 5 days.

SEE IMAGE ON PAGE 47 →

CUSTOMISE YOUR HUMMUS

You can add these ingredients to our Hummus recipe opposite, or you can use a shop-bought hummus. You'll need a food processor or blender for these recipes, in order to achieve a super-smooth, creamy finish.

CHIPOTLE & RED PEPPER HUMMUS

Chipotle is a smoked dried jalapeño that is commonly preserved in adobo sauce. Chipotle paste is widely available and adds a warm, smoky heat that isn't too intense.

SERVES 4 as a starter

400G (14OZ) HUMMUS (shop-bought, or see recipe opposite)

2 TEASPOONS CHIPOTLE PASTE, plus extra to garnish

4 ROASTED RED PEPPERS, sliced (if using jarred, wash and drain well)

1 TEASPOON PAPRIKA

JUICE OF ½ LIME

EXTRA VIRGIN OLIVE OIL, for drizzling

1) Combine all the ingredients in a blender or food processor and blend until completely smooth (3–4 minutes), stopping to scrape down the sides of the blender a couple of times.

2) To serve, scoop into a shallow bowl and create a smooth well in the middle. Drizzle in some oil and garnish with a extra chipotle paste.

CONTINUED OVERLEAF

PEA & HERB HUMMUS

This is a bright green, fresh hummus – perfect for a spring or summer lunch.

SERVES 4 as a starter

50G (1¾OZ) FROZEN PEAS, plus extra, defrosted, to garnish

40G (1½OZ) FLAT-LEAF PARSLEY

40G (1½OZ) FRESH CORIANDER

400G (14OZ) HUMMUS (shop-bought, or see recipe on page 44)

1 TABLESPOON OLIVE OIL

1 TEASPOON AGAVE SYRUP

FRESH MINT LEAVES, to garnish

1) Half fill a small pan with water and bring to the boil over a medium heat. Drop in the peas, parsley and coriander, and cook for 30 seconds, before draining into a colander or sieve and running under a cold tap. Squeeze out the liquid and chop the herbs.

2) Add the peas and herbs to a blender or food processor, along with the hummus, oil and agave. Blend until completely smooth (3–4 minutes), stopping to scrape down the sides of the blender a couple of times.

3) Transfer into a shallow bowl and garnish with a handful of defrosted peas and the fresh mint leaves.

CARROT & TURMERIC HUMMUS

This hummus is more of an autumnal hummus, where the gentle spices complement the carrot, resulting in a beautiful golden dip.

SERVES 4 as a starter

3 TABLESPOONS OLIVE OIL, plus extra for drizzling

2 CARROTS, peeled and sliced into very thin discs (you can use a mandoline for this, if you have one)

½ TEASPOON GROUND TURMERIC

⅛ TEASPOON FENUGREEK LEAVES (methi leaves)

⅛ TEASPOON CUMIN SEEDS

400G (14OZ) HUMMUS (shop-bought, or see recipe on page 44)

JUICE OF ½ ORANGE

_____

To garnish

DILL SPRIGS, chopped

A PINCH OF BLACK ONION SEEDS

1) Heat the olive oil in a frying pan over a medium heat. Add the carrot slices and fry for 5 minutes until starting to colour and soften. Add the turmeric, fenugreek leaves and cumin seeds, and fry for a further 3 minutes.

2) Set aside a few carrot slices for the garnish, then transfer the remainder to a blender or food processor and add the hummus and orange juice. Blend until completely smooth (about 3–4 minutes), stopping to scrape down the sides a couple of times. Add a splash of water if needed.

3) To serve, scoop the hummus into a shallow bowl and create a smooth well in the middle. Drizzle in some olive oil and scatter over the reserved carrot slices, the dill sprigs and the onion seeds to garnish.

chipotle & red pepper hummus →

↙ carrot & turmeric hummus

↗ hummus

← pea & herb hummus

BARBECUE SWEETCORN RIBS

The perfect accompaniment to any summer barbecue spread, these sticky corn ribs will keep both grown-ups and kids happy. The long, thin cut of the ribs really helps them soak up the flavour of the barbecue sauce, and also means they cook quickly on your barbecue or in a griddle pan.

1) Fill a large saucepan with water and add a pinch of salt. Bring to the boil.

2) To prepare the corn ribs, you will need a steady chopping board (anchor it well with a damp cloth underneath to prevent it from slipping) and a very sharp knife. Stand a corn cob up on its end and carefully cut down through the middle of the core, then halve lengthways again. Repeat with the other cobs. If you think you will find this too tricky, you can make shorter ribs by cutting the corn cobs in half widthways first. This makes them less wobbly and easier to cut.

3) Add the ribs to the boiling water and cook for 2 minutes, then place in a sieve under cold running water to stop the cooking.

4) In a large mixing bowl, combine the oil, paprika, garlic and oregano. Add the corn ribs and massage the seasoning mixture into each rib.

5) In another mixing bowl, whisk together the ingredients for the barbecue sauce.

6) Place the ribs on a baking tray and brush them with the barbecue sauce.

7) Preheat your barbecue or heat a griddle pan over a medium–high heat, then grill the ribs for 3–4 minutes on each side, brushing with more barbecue sauce as you go.

8) Place the ribs onto a serving dish and serve with the vegan sour cream, fresh coriander, green chillies and lime wedges for squeezing.

SERVES 4

4 CORNS ON THE COB

1 TABLESPOON OLIVE OIL

1 TEASPOON PAPRIKA

1 GARLIC CLOVE, chopped

1 TEASPOON DRIED OREGANO

SALT

For the barbecue sauce

2 TABLESPOONS TOMATO KETCHUP

1 TABLESPOON SOFT LIGHT BROWN SUGAR

1 TABLESPOON SOY SAUCE OR TAMARI

1 TEASPOON CHIPOTLE PASTE

To serve

VEGAN SOUR CREAM (see page 29)

FRESHLY CHOPPED CORIANDER

SLICED GREEN CHILLIES

LIME WEDGES

TEMPEH LARB

Larb is a fresh Thai dish of spiced mince served with a big plate of herbs and lettuce on the side; you simply spoon the filling into the lettuce cups and roll up, then dip them into the *prik nam pla* dressing. It's a fun, interactive dish to enjoy together. Tempeh carries spice exceptionally well, making it perfect for a vegan version. *Larb* is traditionally served with toasted jasmine rice powder, which you can buy in speciality Asian shops, but we have also included the instructions to make it yourself in the Chef's Tip. If you prefer, you can use crushed roasted peanuts or crispy fried onions for crunch instead.

SERVES 3–4 as a starter

200G (7OZ) TEMPEH, grated on the large side of a box grater

1 TABLESPOON SESAME OIL

1 GARLIC CLOVE, chopped

½ BIRD'S EYE CHILLI, chopped

200G (7OZ) KING OYSTER MUSHROOMS, finely diced

JUICE OF 1 LIME

½ TABLESPOON SOY SAUCE OR TAMARI

1 SMALL SHALLOT, sliced

2 TABLESPOONS CORIANDER STALK, finely chopped

2 SPRING ONIONS, trimmed and finely sliced

For the spice paste

½ LEMON GRASS STALK, tender core only, finely chopped

1 GREEN BIRD'S EYE CHILLI, finely sliced

½ TABLESPOON CUMIN SEEDS

½ TABLESPOON CORIANDER SEEDS

2 THAI LIME LEAVES, deveined and finely chopped

20G (¾OZ) CORIANDER LEAVES, chopped

1 TABLESPOON PALM SUGAR OR SOFT LIGHT BROWN SUGAR

½ TEASPOON SALT

½ TABLESPOON MISO PASTE

To serve

ICEBERG OR BABY GEM LETTUCE LEAVES

THAI BASIL, MINT AND CORIANDER LEAVES

RED CHILLI, diced

TOASTED RICE POWDER (see Chef's Tip), crushed roasted peanuts or crispy fried onions

PRIK NAM PLA (see page 70)

1) Place all the ingredients for the spice paste into a food processor or blender and blend to a smooth paste. Alternatively, combine the ingredients in a pestle and mortar and work to a fine paste.

2) In a mixing bowl, combine the tempeh and spice paste, stirring well to combine.

3) Heat the sesame oil in a wok or large frying pan over a medium heat. Add the garlic and bird's eye chilli, and fry for 2 minutes to infuse the oil, being careful not to burn the garlic.

4) Add the mushrooms and the spiced tempeh. Increase the heat to medium–high and cook for 5 minutes, stirring. Take off the heat and add the lime juice, soy sauce or tamari, shallot, coriander stems and spring onions.

5) Arrange the lettuce, herbs and chilli on a large plate or serving dish. Transfer the larb mixture to a dish or bowl with a spoon and serve alongside a little bowl of the toasted rice (or crushed peanuts or fried onions), and another bowl containing the *Prik Nam Pla*.

6) To eat, take a piece of lettuce and spoon in some larb, then top with your choice of herbs and/or crunchy toppings. Roll the lettuce leaves up loosely, then dip into the *Prik Nam Pla* and enjoy.

CHEF'S TIP

To make the toasted rice powder, place 50g (1¾oz) uncooked jasmine rice and 1 teaspoon peeled grated galangal in a dry frying pan or wok over a low–medium heat. Toast, stirring continually, for about 10 minutes. It will turn a nice brown colour, but don't let it burn. Transfer the fragrant rice to a food processor or a spice grinder and grind to a coarse powder. Alternatively, you can pound it in a pestle and mortar. Sift to remove any large pieces. This will keep in an airtight container for up to 2 weeks.

FILO-WRAPPED ASPARAGUS WITH ROMESCO SAUCE

Filo pastry gives this tender roast asparagus a crunchy finish. You can use any long-stemmed vegetable for this, so Tenderstem broccoli will also work. The romesco sauce will keep for a week in a sealed jar in the fridge and goes with everything from arancini to roast potatoes.

SERVES 4–6

16 MEDIUM-SIZED ASPARAGUS SPEARS, tough ends removed

4 SHEETS OF FILO PASTRY

100G (3½OZ) PLANT-BASED SALTED BUTTER, melted

50G (1¾OZ) VEGAN PARMESAN-STYLE CHEESE, grated

15 BASIL LEAVES, picked

½ TEASPOON FRESHLY GROUND BLACK PEPPER

1 TABLESPOON SEA SALT FLAKES

For the romesco sauce

60G (2¼OZ) FLAKED ALMONDS

2 TABLESPOONS SHERRY VINEGAR

180G (6½OZ) ROASTED RED PEPPERS FROM A JAR, drained and sliced

¼ TEASPOON CASTER SUGAR

1 TEASPOON SMOKED PAPRIKA

100ML (3½FL OZ) OLIVE OIL

4 TABLESPOONS TOMATO PURÉE

¼ TEASPOON SALT

1 TEASPOON CHOPPED FLAT-LEAF PARSLEY LEAVES

1 GARLIC CLOVE, chopped

1) For the romesco sauce, slowly toast the flaked almonds in a small, dry frying pan over a very low heat until fragrant and golden, shaking the pan often to stop them catching. Remove from the pan and set aside on a plate, then return the pan to the heat. Increase the heat to medium–high and add the vinegar. Heat for 2 minutes to cook off most of the liquid, then add the peppers, sugar and paprika. Continue to cook for 3 minutes, stirring slowly. Add the remaining sauce ingredients and cook for a couple of minutes more to break up the purée.

2) Transfer the contents of the pan to a food processor, along with the toasted almonds, and pulse to achieve a chunky paste. Preheat the oven to 180°C/160°C fan/350°F/gas mark 4 and line a baking sheet with baking parchment.

3) Slightly wet a clean cloth or tea towel and wring out well. Remove the filo sheets from the packaging and cover with the damp cloth as you work so it doesn't dry out. Take 1 sheet of filo and brush with melted butter, then scatter over around a third of the vegan Parmesan. Cover with another sheet of filo and brush this sheet with butter. Cut the sheet into quarters so you have 4 rectangles, then cut each one in half again so that you have 8 squares. Repeat with the other 2 filo sheets so you have 16 squares altogether.

4) Sprinkle almost all of the remaining vegan Parmesan, basil and pepper on the bottom halves of all the squares, then, one at a time, place an asparagus spear on the cheesy end of the filo so the tip is poking out. Roll it up quite tightly, then place on the prepared baking sheet. Repeat until all the asparagus is rolled, then give them a final dusting of vegan Parmesan and season.

5) Bake for 10 minutes until crisp and golden, turning halfway so they cook evenly. Serve warm with the romesco sauce.

CHEF'S TIP

Asparagus varies a lot in size. If you have thinner asparagus spears, this will still work. Just cut the filo squares one more time to form 16 rectangles and reduce the cooking time to 8–10 minutes.

PEA, SPINACH & POTATO BONDAS

Cute little gram-flour battered patties, or *bonda*, are a hugely popular street-food snack in India, and a favourite on our menus. They are simple to prepare and a great way to use up leftover cooked potatoes. The filling must be good and firm, so the potatoes need to be starchy and not waterlogged. The peas add a lovely spark of sweetness and colour, and the flavour of the *bonda* is perfect paired with our Mango Pickle Yogurt (see page 182), or with Indian pickles and chutneys.

MAKES 15

250G (9OZ) BABY SPINACH, plus extra to serve

2CM (¾IN) PIECE OF FRESH ROOT GINGER, grated

120G (4¼OZ) FROZEN PEAS OR PETIT POIS

500G (1LB 2OZ) STARCHY POTATOES, boiled in their skins and then peeled

1 SPRING ONION, sliced

60G (2¼OZ) DESICCATED COCONUT

½ TEASPOON SALT

1 GREEN BIRD'S EYE CHILLI, sliced, plus extra to serve

VEGETABLE OR RAPESEED OIL, for frying

MANGO PICKLE YOGURT (see page 182), to serve

For the batter

400G (14OZ) GRAM FLOUR

½ TEASPOON GROUND CUMIN

½ TEASPOON KASHMIRI CHILLI POWDER OR SWEET PAPRIKA

½ TEASPOON GROUND TURMERIC

½ TEASPOON SALT

400ML (14FL OZ) WATER

1) In a food processor, blitz the spinach, ginger and peas. Alternatively, chop well by hand and stir to combine.

2) In a mixing bowl, smash the potatoes, then add the spinach and pea mixture, along with the spring onion, coconut, salt and chilli. Stir everything together to achieve a uniform and solid consistency.

3) In another mixing bowl, prepare the batter by whisking together the gram flour, spices and salt. Slowly pour in the water, whisking all the while, to create a thick, smooth batter.

4) Shape the potato mixture into little patties, each about 40g (1½oz).

5) Pour the oil into a large non-stick frying pan to a depth of 7.5–10cm (3–4in) and place over a medium heat. Heat the oil to 180°C (350°F). If you don't have a cooking thermometer, you can test to see if it's ready by dropping in a little of the batter mixture. The oil should bubble around the batter, but not spit.

6) Working in batches, dip the patties into the batter to coat, then carefully place them into the hot oil. Deep-fry the *bonda* for 5–8 minutes until golden brown, turning over halfway with a slotted spoon. Once crisp and golden on all sides, remove and set aside on a plate lined with kitchen paper to drain any excess oil while you fry the rest.

7) Arrange some baby spinach on a serving dish and top with the *bonda*. Serve with Mango Pickle Yogurt, garnished with sliced green chillies.

WHIPPED AVOCADO, JALAPEÑO & BLACK BEAN QUESADILLAS

Our avocado dip has a fresh, tangy taste and the consistency of loosely whipped cream. It's a perfect light accompaniment to these flavourful bean quesadillas. We've used the oven to finish the quesadillas as it makes them easier to handle and means they are all ready at the same time, but you can prepare them in a frying pan one by one if you prefer.

1) Preheat the oven to 220°C/200°C fan/425°F/ gas mark 7 and line 2 baking trays with baking parchment.

2) To make the whipped avocado cream, pour the oil into a food processor, then add the remaining ingredients, except for the water. Blend the mixture to fully combine, then add the water, a little at a time, blending between each addition to achieve a smooth, creamy consistency. You may not need all the water.

3) To make the quesadillas, heat the oil in a large, non-stick frying pan over a high heat. Add the onion and cook for 2 minutes until translucent, then reduce the heat to medium and add the garlic and red pepper. Cook for 4 minutes, then stir in the spices and cook for a further 1–2 minutes. Finally, add the beans and Tabasco and season to taste with salt, then remove from the heat.

4) Lightly brush one side of a tortilla with oil and place on one of the prepared baking trays, oiled side down. On one half of the tortilla, layer on some cheese, black bean mixture and jalapeño slices, then finish with a little more cheese on top before folding over the tortilla. Repeat with the remaining tortillas and fillings.

5) Press the tortillas down and bake in the oven for 10–15 minutes, or until golden brown.

6) Remove the quesadillas from the oven and cut into wedges before serving with a dollop of the whipped avocado cream.

SERVES 4

2 TABLESPOONS OLIVE OIL, plus extra for brushing

1 ONION, diced

1 GARLIC CLOVE, crushed

1 RED PEPPER, diced

1 PINCH GROUND ALLSPICE

PINCH OF FRESHLY GROUND BLACK PEPPER

½ TEASPOON GROUND CUMIN

400G (14OZ) CAN BLACK BEANS, rinsed and well drained

DASH OF TABASCO

4 × 25CM (10IN) TORTILLAS

200G (7OZ) PLANT-BASED CHEDDAR-STYLE CHEESE, grated

50G (1¾OZ) PICKLED JALAPEÑO CHILLIES

SALT

For the whipped avocado cream

300ML (½ PINT) RAPESEED OIL

5 AVOCADOS, stoned, peeled and halved

JUICE OF 2 LEMONS

50G (1¾OZ) CORIANDER, chopped

50G (1¾OZ) BASIL, chopped

1 TABLESPOON SALT

200ML (7FL OZ) WATER

POTATO & PARSNIP LATKAS

Latkas – delicious, crunchy grated potato cakes – are one of the key traditional foods of Hannukah, the Jewish festival of light. During Hannukah, we eat foods cooked in oil. Latkas make a great supper with sour cream, apple sauce and a salad. They also make a fantastic weekend brunch dish. They can even be served sweet, dipped in cinnamon sugar.

1) Grate the parsnips into a bowl using the large side of a box grater. Add the dill or chives if using and onion, and stir to combine. Set aside.

2) Grate the potatoes into a separate bowl, covering with a tea towel so they don't oxidise. Take a handful of the grated potatoes and squeeze as hard as you can, releasing all the liquid, then add the squeezed potato to the bowl with the parsnips and onions. Continue with the remaining potatoes and stir.

3) Add the baking powder, flour, cornflour or potato starch, pepper flakes, seasoning and coconut yogurt to the bowl. Stir well to combine.

4) Take small handfuls of the mixture, weighing about 80g (2¾oz) each, and roll into balls slightly larger than a ping-pong ball. Repeat until you have used up all the mixture.

5) Pour the oil into a large, deep, non-stick frying pan to a depth of 1cm (½in) and place the pan over a high heat. Heat the oil to 160°C (320°F). If you don't have a cooking thermometer, you can test to see if it's ready by dropping in a little of the latka mixture. The oil should bubble around the mixture, but not spit.

6) Once the oil is ready, cook the latkas in batches. Add the balls to the oil and cook for 3–4 minutes until golden, then press down with a spatula to flatten and cook for 3–4 minutes more. Turn over and cook on the other side for a few more minutes.

7) Remove the latkas from the pan and drain on a wire rack set over a tray while you fry the remaining balls.

8) Serve with the vegan sour cream and apple sauce or cranberry relish.

MAKES 10

175G (6OZ) PARSNIPS, peeled

5 DILL SPRIGS OR CHIVES, chopped (optional)

1 ONION, finely diced

500G (1LB 2OZ) RED POTATOES

1 TABLESPOON BAKING POWDER

60G (2¼OZ) PLAIN FLOUR

30G (1OZ) CORNFLOUR OR POTATO STARCH

½ TEASPOON ALEPPO PEPPER (PUL BIBER) (optional)

1½ TEASPOONS SALT

FRESHLY GROUND BLACK PEPPER

50G (1¾OZ) COCONUT YOGURT

VEGETABLE OIL, for frying

To serve

VEGAN SOUR CREAM (see page 29)

APPLE SAUCE OR CRANBERRY RELISH

BUTTERNUT SQUASH ARANCINI

Arancini are a Sicilian fried snack made by rolling leftover risotto into balls, then coating the risotto balls in breadcrumbs and frying them. They make a great appetiser served with drinks. The risotto recipe below is delicious in its own right, so this is really two dishes in one. Ideally, make the risotto with homemade vegetable stock, but if you don't have time, you can buy a good fresh stock from the supermarket.

MAKES 12

For the risotto

750ML (25FL OZ) VEGETABLE STOCK

2 TABLESPOONS EXTRA VIRGIN OLIVE OIL

1 ONION, finely diced

3 LARGE SAGE LEAVES, chopped

150G (5½OZ) BUTTERNUT SQUASH, cubed

150G (5½OZ) ARBORIO RICE

1 TEASPOON NUTRITIONAL YEAST

100G (3½OZ) VEGAN PARMESAN-STYLE CHEESE, grated

SALT AND FRESHLY GROUND BLACK PEPPER

For the arancini

200G (7OZ) PLAIN FLOUR, plus extra for rolling if needed

PINCH OF SALT

300ML (10½FL OZ) WATER

200G (7OZ) PANKO BREADCRUMBS

RAPESEED OR SUNFLOWER OIL, for frying

10 SAGE LEAVES

To serve

VEGAN AIOLI (see page 170) OR ROMESCO SAUCE
(see page 52)

CONTINUED OVERLEAF →

1) Bring the vegetable stock to the boil in a small saucepan over a medium heat, then reduce the heat so that it is barely simmering.

2) Heat the oil in a heavy-based pan over a low–medium heat. Add the onion and cook gently for 2 minutes until soft and translucent but not coloured.

3) Increase the heat to medium–high and add the sage and butternut squash. Cook for 5 minutes to caramelise the squash, then ladle in about two thirds of the stock. Cover with a lid and cook for 10–12 minutes until the liquid has evaporated and the squash is soft.

4) Smash the butternut squash with a wooden spoon to create a chunky mash, then add the rice and stir until well coated with the squash. Add the remaining stock, a ladleful at a time, adding just enough to cover the rice each time. Keep stirring until the rice has fully absorbed the stock before adding the next ladleful. The rice is ready when it has plumped up and is tender on the outside but retains a slight firmness at the centre (al dente). This will take around 15 minutes.

5) Season with salt and pepper to taste and stir in the nutritional yeast, then take off the heat. The risotto is ready to serve, but if you want to use it to make arancini, it needs to cool completely. Spread the risotto in a thin layer on a tray and put it in the fridge so it cools quickly and doesn't lose its bite.

6) Once the rice is completely cold (this will take about 2 hours), stir in the vegan Parmesan cheese.

7) To shape the arancini, keep a bowl of water close by so you can moisten your hands to help you during the process. Take a couple of tablespoons of rice at a time (around 40g/1½oz) and shape into a ball. Set aside on a plate or tray while you roll the rest. (If you find the mixture is too wet to shape properly, you can roll the balls in a little flour to help.)

8) To make the batter, combine the flour, salt and water in a bowl. Mix thoroughly with a whisk to prevent any lumps from forming. Scatter the panko breadcrumbs on to a plate or into a shallow bowl.

9) Dip the arancini into the batter, one at a time, making sure that you cover them completely, then roll in the panko breadcrumbs to coat.

10) Pour oil into a large saucepan to a depth of 7.5–10cm (3–4in) and place over a medium heat. Heat the oil to 180°C (350°F). If you don't have a cooking thermometer, you can test to see if it's ready by dropping in a small cube of white bread. It should bubble and turn golden, but the oils should not spit or smoke.

11) Fry the arancini one at a time, or two at a time at most, so as not to lower the temperature of the oil by overcrowding the pan. Fry for 5–8 minutes until golden brown, then drain on a plate lined with paper towels while you cook the rest.

12) Turn off the heat and allow the temperature of the oil to come down to 160°C (320°F) (this will take 2–5 minutes), then deep-fry the sage leaves for 2 minutes until crisp.

13) Serve the arancini with the fried sage and a side of aioli or romesco, for dipping.

WHIPPED FETA GARDEN PLATE

Our rich, creamy whipped feta dip is one of those recipes that has multiple uses; it's great with any crunchy vegetables, but also delicious spread over toast or grilled pitta, or even as a dressing for a pasta salad. It really is the gift that keeps on giving. We wanted to give you a dip that you could use as a centrepiece, so dollop it in the centre of your nicest serving dish or plate and arrange the colourful crudités around it in a random fashion, building them up for a 'garden' effect. We've added some suggestions for crudités, but use anything seasonal, tasty and pretty.

1) To make the whipped feta, crumble the vegan feta into the bowl of a stand mixer and beat with the paddle attachment for 5 minutes. Add the remaining ingredients one at the time, beating between each addition, until everything is well combined and the mixture has a smooth, creamy consistency. If you don't have a stand mixer, you can use a food processor – or, to do it by hand, simply crumble the vegan feta into a bowl, mash well with a whisk, then pour in the oil and plant-based cream. Whisk well, then stir in the remaining ingredients with a spatula.

2) Scoop the whipped feta into the middle of a serving plate and arrange the veggies around it, then garnish with olives and almonds and serve.

SEE IMAGE, OVERLEAF

SERVES 4–6

250G (9OZ) VEGAN FETA-STYLE CHEESE

1 TABLESPOON OLIVE OIL

ZEST OF 1 LEMON

150ML (5FL OZ) PLANT-BASED CREAM

½ TEASPOON SALT

PINCH OF FRESHLY GROUND BLACK PEPPER

Crudités suggestions

3 CARROTS, cut into batons

3 RADISHES, leaves left on

6 FRENCH BREAKFAST RADISHES, leaves left on

500G (1LB 2OZ) ASPARAGUS, blanched

LEBANESE CUCUMBERS, cut in half lengthways

10 CHERRY TOMATOES

LETTUCE LEAVES

SUGAR-SNAP PEAS, cut in half lengthways

To serve

10 GOOD-QUALITY MIXED OLIVES

SMALL HANDFUL OF SALTED BLANCHED ALMONDS

CORONATION CHICKPEA SALAD CUPS

We've presented this as salad cups, but our coronation chickpeas also make a kickass filling for wraps or sandwiches. The flavour of the chickpeas relies on the quality of the mango chutney; the type we like is spiked with lots of nigella seeds and cardamom.

1) In a large, non-reactive bowl, combine all the ingredients for the coronation chickpeas. Using a fork, slightly crush the chickpeas, then whisk everything together to combine. Leave to marinate for at least 30 minutes.

2) Meanwhile, in a separate bowl, combine all the ingredients for the mango salsa.

3) To serve, arrange the lettuce leaves on a large platter and scoop some of the coronation chickpeas evenly into each one. Top with the salsa, followed by some radish slices, then scatter over some more green chilli and finish with a sprinkle of toasted flaked almonds or a crunchy Indian garnish like sev (fried noodles).

SERVES 4–6 as a starter

250G (9OZ) CANNED CHICKPEAS, washed and drained

1 TABLESPOON GOOD-QUALITY COLD-PRESSED RAPESEED OIL

1 TEASPOON TIKKA CURRY POWDER

1 TABLESPOON MANGO CHUTNEY

2 SPRING ONIONS, finely chopped

JUICE AND ZEST OF ½ LIME

1 TABLESPOON FRESH CORIANDER, chopped

1 TEASPOON GREEN CHILLI, finely chopped, plus extra to serve

2 TABLESPOONS VEGAN MAYO (shop-bought, or see our recipe on page 170)

PINCH OF SALT

For the mango salsa

¼ MANGO, peeled and finely diced

¼ CUCUMBER, deseeded and finely diced

½ GREEN CHILLI, finely diced

PINCH OF SALT

To serve

1 HEAD ROUND OR BUTTER LETTUCE, leaves separated

2 RADISHES, finely sliced

2–3 TABLESPOONS TOASTED FLAKED ALMONDS OR SPICED SEV (fried noodles – see page 11)

light

SALMOREJO WITH CUCUMBER SALSA

Salmorejo is a cold soup from Andalusia in Spain. It's like gazpacho, but thicker and creamier. The velvety texture is a result of the combination of bread and olive oil. We serve this with a cucumber salsa to add a spark of colour, crunch and freshness. This makes a nice, light starter, but is also great served in little glasses as a canapé or amuse bouche.

SERVES 4 (or 8 as a canapé)

400G (14OZ) WHITE BREAD

1KG (2LB 4OZ) RIPE SEASONAL TOMATOES, roughly chopped

1 CUCUMBER, roughly chopped

1 RED ONION, roughly chopped

2 GARLIC CLOVES, grated

100ML (3½FL OZ) WHITE WINE VINEGAR

150ML (¼ PINT) WATER

4 TABLESPOONS EXTRA VIRGIN OLIVE OIL

1 TEASPOON SALT

For the cucumber salsa

200G (7OZ) CUCUMBER, *deseeded and finely diced*

1 SHALLOT, *finely diced*

1 TEASPOON FINELY CHOPPED FLAT-LEAF PARSLEY

½ TEASPOON SALT

1 TABLESPOON EXTRA VIRGIN OLIVE OIL, plus a little extra for drizzling

JUICE OF ½ LEMON

1) Crumble the bread into a food processor or blender, then add all the remaining ingredients for the *salmorejo*. Blend until completely smooth. The consistency should be like a thick tomato soup. If it is too thick, add some more water.

2) To make the cucumber salsa, combine the diced cucumber, shallot and parsley in a small bowl. Season with the salt, oil and lemon juice.

3) Ladle the *salmorejo* into individual bowls or glasses, then top with the salsa. Finish with a drizzle of extra virgin olive oil.

GRILLED PEACH & TOMATO SALAD WITH THAI BASIL

In a salad like this, the produce is the star of the show, so look for seasonal peaches and tomatoes that are sweet and ripe, but still firm enough to cut into clean halves. Thai basil (similar to holy basil) has a delicate aniseed flavour that pairs really well with the peaches here. The *Prik Nam Pla*, or Thai chilli dipping sauce, draws out the natural sweetness of the fruit. We have used miso here in place of the traditional fish sauce to add a similar salty, fermented depth of flavour.

SERVES 4–6

4–5 RIPE PEACHES, pitted, halved and cut into wedges

500G (1LB 2OZ) RIPE SEASONAL TOMATOES (preferably a mixture of shapes and sizes)

15G (½OZ) THAI BASIL, leaves picked

PINCH OF SALT

1 TABLESPOON TOASTED SESAME OIL

3–4 RADISHES, finely sliced, to garnish

For the prik nam pla

JUICE OF 3 LIMES

1 TEASPOON MISO PASTE

½ TEASPOON SALT

1 TABLESPOON PALM SUGAR OR MAPLE SYRUP

4 GARLIC CLOVES, finely chopped

2 BIRD'S EYE CHILLIES, finely sliced

1) To make the *Prik Nam Pla*, combine all the ingredients in a jar and shake until the sugar has dissolved. Set aside.

2) Preheat a barbecue to high or place a griddle pan over a high heat. Grill the peach wedges for 1–2 minutes without moving them, so clear grill lines are formed, then turn over and do the same on the other side. Take them off the grill and allow to cool a little.

3) Combine the peaches and tomatoes in a large bowl, along with half the Thai basil leaves. Dress with the *Prik Nam Pla*, then season with salt and drizzle over the sesame oil.

4) Arrange the dressed salad on a plate or serving dish. Garnish with the remining basil leaves and the radish slices, and serve.

AMBA CHICK'N KEBABS

Our Amba Chick'n Kebabs have been a bestseller for years now. The sour, sweet amba pickle loves to be charred and results in great grill marks and caramelisation on the plant-based chick'n. The chick'n needs to marinate for at least an hour, but overnight is even better. These kebabs make a great addition to a barbecue spread, and are also a delicious light dinner served with our Lemon Cashew Rice (see page 159) or Shirazi Salad (see page 142). We also like to serve this with a little more amba and some Whipped Tahini (see page 176).

MAKES 8 (serves 2 as a main, or 4 as part of a spread)

160G (5¾OZ) PLANT-BASED CHICK'N PIECES

4 TABLESPOONS AMBA (shop-bought, or use our Quick Amba recipe on page 169)

1 TABLESPOON COCONUT YOGURT

2 RED ONIONS, cut into wedges

½ RED PEPPER (we like to use pointed peppers for this), deseeded and cut into chunks

½ SMALL COURGETTE, cut into chunks

You will also need 8 wooden kebab skewers pre-soaked in water, or 8 metal skewers.

1) In a bowl, combine the chick'n pieces with the amba and yogurt. Cover and leave to marinate for at least 1 hour in the fridge (overnight would be great).

2) To assemble the kebabs, skewer the chunks of onion, pepper and courgette, alternating with the chick'n pieces (each skewer should have 2–3 pieces of chick'n, depending on the size).

3) Preheat the barbecue to medium–high or place a griddle pan over a medium–high heat. Cook the skewers for 3–5 minutes on each side, turning twice as they cook, to form clear char marks and heat the chick'n all the way through. Serve piping hot off the grill.

BÁNH XÈO

Bánh xèo, which translates from the Vietnamese as 'sizzling pancakes', are thin, crispy crêpes stuffed with fresh, crunchy fillings. They're a common street food in Vietnam. We suggest you serve the salad in a big bowl on the table, and let people fill up the crêpes themselves. Always serve these gluten-free pancakes hot and fresh from the pan, as they become crumbly when they cool.

1) Prepare the salad first. In a salad bowl, whisk together the lime juice, agave, soy sauce or tamari and red chilli. Add the remaining salad ingredients and toss to combine, then set aside.

2) To make the crêpe batter, combine the flour, turmeric, salt and sugar in a food processor or blender, then add the coconut milk and water and blend to form a thick, smooth batter the consistency of thick cream. (You can do this by hand if you prefer.)

3) Heat the oil in a non-stick frying pan or a flat crêpe pan over a medium–high heat. Add a generous amount of the crêpe batter; enough to cover the base of the whole pan in a thin layer. While the mixture is setting, sprinkle over some of the spring onions and chilli. Cook for 2–4 minutes until the edges are crisp and golden, and bubbles are forming all over the pancake. Flip and cook on the other side for 1 minute, then remove from the pan and serve to your guests straight away with the salad while you cook the next crêpe.

SEE IMAGE, OVERLEAF ➤

MAKES 6–7 LARGE CRÊPES

500G (1LB 2OZ) RICE FLOUR

½ TEASPOON GROUND TURMERIC

1 TEASPOON SALT

1 TEASPOON CASTER SUGAR

500ML (18FL OZ) COCONUT MILK

400ML (14FL OZ) WATER

2 TABLESPOONS VEGETABLE OR RAPESEED OIL

4 SPRING ONIONS, finely sliced

1 RED CHILLI, diced

_____

For the salad

3 TABLESPOONS LIME JUICE

1 TABLESPOON AGAVE SYRUP

1 TABLESPOON SOY SAUCE OR TAMARI

1 TEASPOON SLICED RED CHILLI

1 HEAD BUTTER LETTUCE OR SIMILAR, leaves separated

10 CORIANDER SPRIGS, leaves picked

10 MINT SPRIGS, leaves picked

½ CUCUMBER, halved lengthways then thinly sliced

50G (1¾OZ) BEANSPROUTS

SPICED TAHINI AUBERGINES WITH BRINJAL PICKLE YOGURT & MANGO SALAD

Sweet, tangy brinjal pickle is one of the most popular Indian condiments. *Brinjal* means 'aubergine', so this is really a double aubergine recipe. These work really well on a barbecue, but you can still achieve the desired smoky, charred flavour with a griddle pan. The fresh mango salad offsets the smoky flavour of the aubergine by adding some freshness and acidity.

SERVES 4

2 AUBERGINES

2 TABLESPOONS TAHINI

4 TABLESPOONS VEGETABLE OIL

2 GARLIC CLOVES, finely chopped

1 TABLESPOON MEDIUM CURRY POWDER (look for one with fenugreek leaves, also known as methi)

½ TEASPOON SALT

INDIAN SNACK MIX SUCH AS SEV (fried noodles – see page 11) OR COCONUT FLAKES, to serve (optional)

For the brinjal pickle yogurt

4 CARDAMOM PODS

350G (12OZ) COCONUT YOGURT

100G (3½OZ) BRINJAL PICKLE

JUICE OF 1 LIME

½ RED BIRD'S EYE CHILLI, very finely chopped

1 TABLESPOON VERY FINELY CHOPPED CORIANDER

For the mango salad

2 MANGOS, diced

½ RED BIRD'S EYE CHILLI, chopped

JUICE OF 1 LIME

HANDFUL OF CORIANDER, chopped

1 TEASPOON OLIVE OIL

½ TEASPOON SALT

1 TABLESPOON CHOPPED MINT LEAVES

CONTINUED OVERLEAF →

1) Using a vegetable peeler, peel the aubergines lengthways to create stripes. Halve both aubergines lengthways and score the flesh with the tip of a sharp knife to create a diamond crosshatch pattern about 2.5cm (1in) deep. Be careful not to pierce the skin.

2) In a bowl, whisk together the tahini and vegetable oil. Add the garlic and curry powder and stir. Pour this mixture over the aubergines and massage so that all the liquid and spices goes into the cuts you've made.

3) Heat a barbecue to medium–high or place a griddle pan over a medium–high heat. Once hot, grill the aubergines, skin-side down, for 4 minutes, then turn over and grill on the over side for 15 minutes. If you're using a barbecue with a lid, close the lid so the aubergines absorb the flavour of the smoke as they grill. The aubergines should be deeply marked but not burned and the flesh should be soft.

4) Meanwhile, prepare the brinjal pickle yogurt. Break open the cardamom pods and crush the seeds. Place the yogurt in a mixing bowl and stir in the cardamom seeds, followed by all the other ingredients. Set aside.

5) Once the aubergines are ready, let them rest for 5 minutes.

6) Meanwhile, make the mango salad by mixing all the ingredients together in a large bowl.

7) To serve, plate up each aubergine half topped with 2 tablespoons of the brinjal pickle yogurt and 2 tablespoons of mango salad. If you like, you can finish by scattering over a crunchy snack mix like sev (fried noodles) or coconut flakes.

FREGOLA FETA COURGETTES

Fregola is a tasty Sardinian pasta made from hard durum wheat flour that has been rolled, sun-dried and toasted to a mix of yellow, gold and brown shades. Also known as giant couscous, it can be cooked in a similar way to risotto rice, simmered in stock, or even boiled, drained and dressed like a salad. It gets better as it sits, absorbing the cooking liquid and swelling with flavour. The vegan feta-style cheese used here adds some sharpness and saltiness to the dish, which is rounded out with fresh torn basil leaves and baby cherry tomatoes.

1) Heat the oil in a large non-stick frying pan over a high heat. Add the bay leaf, garlic and courgette and cook for 2 minutes to get some colour on the courgette slices.

2) Add the turmeric and fregola and toast for 2 minutes, then reduce the heat to low–medium. Add the stock, a ladleful at a time, adding just enough to cover the fregola. Keep stirring, and once the fregola has absorbed all the stock, add the next ladleful. After 15–18 minutes, the fregola should be tender, but still with a little bite.

3) Remove the pan from the heat, then stir in the tomatoes, basil and lemon zest and juice. Taste and season if needed.

4) Crumble the vegan feta on top of the fregola, scatter over a few torn basil leaves, and serve.

SERVES 2

3 TABLESPOONS EXTRA VIRGIN OLIVE OIL

1 BAY LEAF

3 GARLIC CLOVES, finely chopped

1 COURGETTE, sliced into thin rounds

¼ TEASPOON GROUND TURMERIC

200G (7OZ) FREGOLA

550ML (18½FL OZ) VEGETABLE STOCK

200G (7OZ) BABY PLUM TOMATOES, halved

15G (½OZ) BASIL, chopped, plus a few extra leaves for garnish

ZEST OF 1 LEMON AND JUICE OF ½

80G (2¾OZ) VEGAN FETA-STYLE CHEESE, crumbled

SALT AND FRESHLY GROUND BLACK PEPPER

VIETNAMESE-STYLE PULLED OYSTER MUSHROOM SALAD

This is our take on the classic Vietnamese chicken salad *goi ga*, replacing the chicken with pulled or shredded king oyster mushrooms. Oyster mushrooms are particularly useful in plant-based cooking, as they have a mild taste but a meaty texture that holds flavour well. Paired with this crunchy fragrant salad and its acidic dressing, the result is a satisfying dish that's full of flavour.

SERVES 2

300G (10½OZ) KING OYSTER MUSHROOMS, grated on the large side of a box grater

1 TEASPOON SMOKED PAPRIKA

1 TABLESPOON TOASTED SESAME OIL

1 TABLESPOON HOI SIN SAUCE

SALT AND FRESHLY GROUND BLACK PEPPER

For the dressing

ZEST AND JUICE OF 2 LIMES

1 TEASPOON MISO PASTE

1 TABLESPOON CASTER SUGAR

½ TEASPOON SALT

1 BIRD'S EYE CHILLI (RED OR GREEN), sliced

1 GARLIC CLOVE, finely grated

For the salad

¼ DAIKON (ABOUT 150G/5½OZ), julienned

2 CARROTS, julienned, or 80G (2¾OZ) CARROT & LIME LEAF PICKLES (see page 185)

1 SMALL CUCUMBER, halved lengthways then sliced at an angle

4 SPRING ONIONS, finely sliced

1 TABLESPOON TORN MINT LEAVES

100G (3½OZ) CORIANDER, torn

To garnish

HANDFUL OF PISTACHIOS, chopped

EDIBLE FLOWERS (optional)

1) In a large bowl, combine the oyster mushrooms with the smoked paprika, then season with salt and pepper.

2) Heat the sesame oil in a frying pan or wok over a medium heat. Add the mushrooms and sauté for 3 minutes, then add the hoi sin sauce. Stir and cook for 3 more minutes, until the mixture is thick and fragrant. Season to taste, then set aside.

3) To prepare the dressing, combine all the ingredients in a jar or bowl and shake or stir well until the sugar has dissolved.

4) For the salad, combine the julienned vegetables in a large bowl, then add the cucumber, spring onions, mint and coriander. Pour over the dressing and toss to combine.

5) Divide the salad between 2 bowls, then top with the warm oyster mushroom mixture. Garnish with a sprinkle of chopped pistachios, and some edible flowers, if you like.

SINGAPORE NOODLES

Singapore noodles are unlikely to have actually originated in Singapore; they are thought to have been the creation of the Cantonese community living in San Francisco. Regardless of its origins, this dish is a quick, delicious stir-fry that can be ready in minutes and is easy to prepare at home. One of our head chefs, Chee, brought this dish to our menus. The key is to have everything ready before you start – and to use a smoking-hot wok.

1) The best way to prepare the rice noodles is to soak them overnight in plenty of cold water. Alternatively, you can bring a kettle of water to the boil, then wait 2 minutes before pouring it into a large bowl. Add the rice noodles and soak for a few minutes until soft, then drain and drizzle with sesame oil to stop them sticking together.

2) To make the Singapore spice mix, combine all the ingredients in a small bowl and mix well.

3) Heat the sesame oil in a wok over a high heat. Add the Chinese cabbage or pak choi, sugar snap peas and pepper, and stir-fry for 2 minutes. Add the spring onions, carrot and soy sauce or tamari and stir-fry for another 2 minutes.

4) Continue to stir-fry as you add 2 teaspoons of the spice mix, along with the scrambled tofu, bean sprouts and the cooked noodles. Cook for 1 more minute, stirring, until everything is combined.

5) Divide the noodles between 2 bowls and serve drizzled with sesame oil and topped with red chilli slices, chopped coriander, sliced spring onions and crispy fried onions.

CHEF'S TIP

To save time, you can use a 250g (9oz) bag of prepared stir-fry vegetables.

Leftover spice mix can be kept in an airtight container for up to 2 weeks.

SERVES 2

100G (3½OZ) DRIED RICE VERMICELLI NOODLES

50ML (2FL OZ) SESAME OIL, plus extra for drizzling

¼ SMALL CHINESE CABBAGE OR PAK CHOI (ABOUT 110G/4OZ), sliced

ABOUT 10 SUGAR SNAP PEAS, sliced

½ RED PEPPER, sliced

3–4 SPRING ONIONS, sliced

½ CARROT, sliced into julienne strips

1 TABLESPOON SOY SAUCE OR TAMARI

125G (4½OZ) RED PEPPER ONE-PAN SCRAMBLED TOFU (see page 24, but do not add the cream), or crumbled tofu seasoned with 1 teaspoon *kala namak* (black salt), ¼ teaspoon ground turmeric and black pepper

100G (3½OZ) BEAN SPROUTS

For the Singapore spice mix

½ TABLESPOON CURRY POWDER

½ TEASPOON SOFT LIGHT BROWN SUGAR

¼ TEASPOON GROUND WHITE PEPPER

¼ TEASPOON GROUND TURMERIC

⅛ TEASPOON GROUND ALL SPICE

¼ TEASPOON SALT

To serve

SLICED RED CHILLIES

CHOPPED CORIANDER

SLICED SPRING ONIONS

CRISPY FRIED ONIONS

PASTA CRUDAIOLA

Fresh, simple and rich, this pasta salad can be eaten straight away or stored in the fridge for later (it will keep for up to 1 day). We chose orecchiette (little ears), a typical Puglian pasta, because its firm texture holds an oily sauce like rocket pesto well, allowing the flavour to soak in while retaining its bite. If you haven't got time to make the rocket pesto, you can use a shop-bought vegan pesto, but the bitterness of the rocket works exceptionally well in this dish.

SERVES 2

300G (10½OZ) CHERRY OR BABY PLUM TOMATOES, quartered

30G (1OZ) CAPERS IN VINEGAR, drained

½ SMALL RED ONION, finely diced

4 TABLESPOONS EXTRA VIRGIN OLIVE OIL

¼ TEASPOON MILD CHILLI POWDER

½ TEASPOON SALT

200G (7OZ) DRIED ORECCHIETTE PASTA

2½ TABLESPOONS ROCKET & HAZELNUT PESTO (see page 177)

1) In a large serving dish or salad bowl, combine the tomatoes, capers, red onion, olive oil, chilli powder and salt.

2) Bring a large, well-salted pan of water to the boil, and cook the orecchiette according to the packet instructions to achieve an al dente finish.

3) Drain well and combine with the rocket pesto, then tip into the bowl with the tomato mixture and toss to combine before serving.

SMOKY CHICKPEA COBB SALAD

Americans do big satisfying salads really well, and this vegan version of the classic cobb is just that. The smoky chickpeas give a protein-packed, delicious finish to the salad and contrast perfectly with the crunchy vegetables and mint vinaigrette.

1) First prepare the vinaigrette. Combine all the ingredients in a blender and blend until smooth. Alternatively, combine them in a jug and use a stick blender.

2) To make the smoky chickpeas, heat the oil in a non-stick frying over a medium heat. Add the chickpeas and cook for a minute or two before adding the bacon glaze. Cook for 1 minute more until all the bacon glaze has been absorbed and the chickpeas have a glossy brown sheen.

3) Separate the lettuce leaves and arrange them in a large salad bowl along with the artichoke hearts, tomatoes, onion, sweetcorn, red pepper and avocado. Pour over enough vinaigrette to give the salad a good coating and toss to combine (if you don't use it all, the vinaigrette will keep in the fridge for up to 5 days). Top with the smoky chickpeas, then scatter over the chives and serve with Za'atar Pitta Chips, if you like.

SERVES 2–3

200G (7OZ) ROMAINE, COS OR LITTLE GEM LETTUCE

100G (3½OZ) JARRED ARTICHOKE HEARTS, drained and sliced

125G (4½OZ) CHERRY TOMATOES, halved

¼ RED ONION, finely sliced

100G (3½OZ) FROZEN SWEETCORN

1 POINTED RED PEPPER, diced

1 SMALL AVOCADO, pitted, peeled and sliced

CHOPPED CHIVES, for sprinkling

ZA'ATAR PITTA CHIPS (see page 162), to serve (optional)

For the vinaigrette

150ML (¼ PINT) OLIVE OIL

100ML (3½FL OZ) CIDER VINEGAR

½ TEASPOON SALT

1½ TABLESPOONS AGAVE SYRUP

2 MINT SPRIGS, leaves picked (about 10 leaves)

FRESHLY GROUND BLACK PEPPER

For the smoky chickpeas

1 TABLESPOON OLIVE OIL

125G (4½OZ) CANNED CHICKPEAS, rinsed and drained

4–5 TABLESPOONS BACON GLAZE (see page 31)

GYOZA IN SHIITAKE MISO BROTH

Broths or *dashi* are a key component of Japanese cuisine, and are often cooked slowly over long periods of time. This recipe uses dried shiitake mushrooms; due to their intense, rich flavour and meaty texture, you can achieve a umami-packed miso broth in just 15 minutes. There are many types of gyoza, or Japanese dumplings, available to buy from the freezer department of good shops. This recipe will complement most flavours of vegetable gyoza.

SERVES 2

20G (¾OZ) DRIED SHIITAKE MUSHROOMS

1 LITRE BOILING WATER

2 TABLESPOONS SESAME OIL

1 GARLIC CLOVE, grated

2.5CM (1IN) PIECE OF FRESH ROOT GINGER, peeled and finely grated

80G (2¾OZ) MIXED MUSHROOMS, sliced (we recommend a mixture of oyster, shiitake and enoki)

10 SHOP-BOUGHT VEGETABLE GYOZA

1 TABLESPOON WHITE MISO PASTE

2 TABLESPOONS SOY SAUCE OR TAMARI

1 TABLESPOON MIRIN

PINCH OF DRIED CHILLI FLAKES

To serve

2 SPRING ONIONS, finely sliced

50G (1¾OZ) BAMBOO SHOOTS

TOASTED SESAME SEEDS OR *FURIKAKE* (RICE SEASONING), to garnish

1) Place the dried shiitake in a large bowl and pour over the boiling water. Leave to soak for about 10 minutes until the shiitake are rehydrated.

2) Heat the oil in a large saucepan over a medium heat. Add the garlic and ginger and cook for 30 seconds until light golden, then add the fresh mushrooms and cook for another 5 minutes until the mushrooms are golden and tender.

3) Meanwhile, drain the shiitake, reserving the soaking liquor. Slice the rehydrated shiitake into thin strips and add these to the pan, along with the soaking liquor. Bring to a steady simmer, then add the vegetable gyoza. Increase the heat to high and cook for 4–5 minutes, at a steady simmer but not a rolling boil.

4) Check if the dumplings are cooked all the way through, then turn off the heat and add the white miso, soy sauce or tamari, mirin and chilli flakes. Stir gently until the miso is completely dissolved.

5) Add the spring onions and bamboo shoots to the broth, then divide between 2 bowls. Finish with a sprinkling of toasted sesame seeds or *furikake*.

HISPI CASHEW MOILEE

Moilee is a creamy and mild coconut curry from Goa. It pairs fantastically well with tender cabbage like hispi, or pointed cabbage. The sauce is so simple; you really must use fresh curry leaves, though, as they are carrying the bulk of the flavour. They are available from any shop with a decent range of Indian ingredients, and once you buy them, you can store them in the freezer. Serve this with warm vegan naan or paratha to mop up the sauce, or basmati rice. This is also great served with our Toasted Coconut Rice (see page 161).

1) Heat the oil in a large saucepan over a medium heat. Add the onion, ginger, garlic and curry leaves. Cook for 8–10 minutes, or until softened, stirring regularly.

2) Stir in the chilli, black mustard seeds and turmeric, and cook for 1 minute, then add the coconut milk, creamed coconut and salt. Bring to a simmer, then cook for 10 minutes until the coconut cream has completely dissolved.

3) Meanwhile, melt the butter in a frying pan over a medium heat. Add the cabbage quarters and cook for 4 minutes on one cut side, then turn and cook on the other cut side for another 4 minutes. Add a splash of boiling water to the pan and cover with a lid; once all the water is evaporated and the cabbage is tender, add the cumin seeds and cook for 2 minutes more. Season to taste.

4) Place the cabbage in a deep serving dish and pour over the *moilee* sauce. Scatter over the toasted cashews and finish with some fresh coriander. Serve with lime halves on the side for squeezing.

CHEF'S TIP

This hispi works really well on the barbecue. To prepare, blanch the cabbage for 30 seconds in rapidly boiling salted water, then drain. Toss in oil and cumin seeds, then season before grilling on both sides.

SERVES 4

2 TABLESPOONS LIGHT OIL, such as rapeseed or vegetable oil

1 ONION, diced

3CM (1¼IN) PIECE FRESH ROOT GINGER, peeled and finely grated

4 GARLIC CLOVES, finely chopped

6 FRESH CURRY LEAVES

1 RED BIRD'S EYE CHILLI, finely chopped

½ TABLESPOON BLACK MUSTARD SEEDS

1 TEASPOON GROUND TURMERIC

400ML (14FL OZ) CAN COCONUT MILK

100G (3½OZ) CREAMED COCONUT, grated

1 TEASPOON SALT, plus extra to taste

2 TABLESPOONS PLANT-BASED BUTTER

1 LARGE OR 2 SMALL HISPI CABBAGE(S), quartered lengthways

½ TEASPOON CUMIN SEEDS

FRESHLY GROUND BLACK PEPPER

To serve

50G (1¾OZ) TOASTED CASHEW NUTS

CORIANDER LEAVES, chopped

LIME HALVES

comfort

SALT & PEPPER TOFU

Jiao yan is a classic Cantonese salt-and-pepper seasoning that's delicious with tofu. The pepper used is not black pepper but Sichuan, which has a different kind of heat and results in a tingly, mouth-numbing sensation. You can buy the seasoning mix online or from any shop with a decent selection of Chinese ingredients, but we have included a recipe to make it yourself if you wish. The salt-and-pepper mix is perfect with firm tofu, resulting in a crunchy, fragrant but slightly spicy exterior, and a pillowy soft centre. Usually the tofu is served alone, with just the chilli and garlic, but we've added a stir-fry vegetable mix to turn this into a bright, filling meal.

1) To make the salt-and-pepper mix, warm the spices in a dry frying pan over a low heat until fragrant. Transfer to a pestle and mortar or spice grinder. Add the salt and pound or grind to a fine crumb.

2) To prepare the tofu, combine the cornflour and 2 teaspoons of the salt-and-pepper mixture in a large bowl. Add the tofu cubes and toss to coat.

3) Pour the oil into a large wok to a depth of 1cm (½in) and place over a medium heat. Heat the oil to 180°C (350°F). If you don't have a cooking thermometer, you can test to see if it's ready by dropping in a little of the cornflour mixture. It should bubble, but not spit. Add the seasoned tofu and fry for about 10 minutes, turning the pieces regularly to make sure all the sides are crisp and well coated. Remove from the wok with a slotted spoon and set aside on a plate lined with kitchen paper.

4) Return the wok to the heat and add more oil if necessary. Add the garlic and chilli, followed by the onion, red and green peppers and choi sum or bok choi. Scatter over 1 teaspoon of the salt-and-pepper mixture and add the sesame oil, then increase the heat to high and fry, tossing often, for a minute or two until the vegetables begin to catch. Add the spring onions and stir-fry for 1 minute more.

5) Return the tofu to the pan and toss through, then serve with rice, garnished with the chopped coriander leaves.

SERVES 2

50G (1¾OZ) CORNFLOUR

325G (11½OZ) FIRM TOFU, drained and pressed or dried with a piece of kitchen paper, sliced into 16 cubes

RAPESEED OIL, for frying

4 GARLIC CLOVES, chopped

1 TEASPOON RED CHILLI, diced

1 ONION, sliced

100G (3½OZ) RED PEPPER, cored and cut into thick strips

100G (3½OZ) GREEN PEPPER, cored and cut into thick strips

100G (3½OZ) CHOI SUM OR BOK CHOI, stems sliced into 3–4cm (1¼–1½in) batons

SPLASH OF SESAME OIL

3 SPRING ONIONS, each cut into 3cm (1¼in) lengths

STEAMED RICE, to serve

10 CORIANDER SPRIGS, leaves picked and roughly chopped

For the salt-and-pepper mix

½ TEASPOON GROUND OR 1 TEASPOON WHOLE SICHUAN PEPPERCORNS

½ STAR ANISE

½ TEASPOON SESAME SEEDS

¼ TEASPOON FENNEL SEEDS

4 TEASPOONS SALT

CHILLI MISO BUTTER UDON

Requiring just five minutes and one pot, this is a deliciously quick dinner with minimal washing-up. Prepared udon usually comes in pre-packed portions of 200g (7oz), so this recipe serves one but can easily be multiplied. Gochujang has a warm, medium heat, but if you don't like spice, you can replace the gochujang with regular red or white miso paste.

SERVES 1

1 TABLESPOON GOCHUJANG PASTE

½ TABLESPOON SOY SAUCE OR TAMARI

1 TABLESPOON SESAME OIL

80G (2¾OZ) TENDERSTEM BROCCOLI, trimmed and cut into 2cm (¾in) slices

200G (7OZ) UDON NOODLES

1 GARLIC CLOVE, grated

6 SHIITAKE MUSHROOMS, cut into razor-thin slivers

1 TABLESPOON PLANT-BASED BUTTER

LARGE HANDFUL OF BABY SPINACH

2 SPRING ONIONS, very finely sliced

SALT

1) In a small bowl, combine the gochujang, soy sauce or tamari and sesame oil.

2) Bring a large pan of salted water to the boil over a medium heat. Add the broccoli and udon noodles and cook for 3 minutes.

3) Drain the noodles and broccoli and return to the pan, still over a medium heat. Add the garlic and mushrooms, along with the gochujang mixture and butter. Cook for 1 minute, stirring to combine.

4) Stir in the spinach, then transfer to a bowl and serve, topped with the spring onions.

BOKKEUMBAP

The Korean-style fried rice *bokkeumbap* has been a firm favourite on our menu for years. It's a great use for leftover rice, and we use kimchi and tofu puffs to turn it into a filling and flavourful meal. The key is to have everything prepared in advance. Wok cooking should always be fast, taking just 3–4 minutes to complete the dish, so preparation is everything.

SERVES 2

2 TABLESPOONS SESAME OIL

2 GARLIC CLOVES, crushed or finely grated

1 SMALL ONION, sliced

⅛ TEASPOON DRIED CHILLI FLAKES

200G (7OZ) VEGAN KIMCHI, chopped

3 SPRING ONIONS, sliced into 2.5cm (1in) lengths

300G (10½OZ) COOKED LONG-GRAIN RICE

40G (1½OZ) BEAN SPROUTS

8 TOFU PUFFS (see page 11), halved

50G (1¾OZ) KOREAN-STYLE GLAZE (see page 179)

To serve

CRISPY FRIED ONIONS

FINELY SLICED SPRING ONIONS

NORI FLAKES

FURIKAKE (RICE SEASONING) OR TOASTED SESAME SEEDS

1) Heat the sesame oil in a wok or heavy-based frying pan over a high heat. Add the garlic, onion and chilli flakes, and stir-fry for 1 minute until the onions and garlic are light brown.

2) Add the kimchi and spring onions and stir-fry for a couple more minutes, then add the rice. Continue to stir-fry for another 3–5 minutes, the add the bean sprouts, tofu puffs and Korean-Style Glaze. Cook for a further 2 minutes, stirring all the while.

3) Remove from the heat and serve immediately, garnished with crispy onions, spring onions, nori flakes and *furikake* or toasted sesame seeds.

CHEF'S TIP

If you don't want to use tofu puffs, then shredded plant-based chick'n works really well.

SWEET POTATO MAC & CHEEZ

A great-tasting vegan cheese sauce is a handy recipe to have at your disposal – in addition to this delicious Mac and Cheez, it can also be used as a warm dip for nachos. We add a little chipotle for smokiness, but if you prefer, try it with the same amount of red miso for depth of flavour without the spice.

1) Preheat the oven to 200°C/180°C fan/400°F/ gas mark 6 and line a baking sheet with baking parchment. Toss the sweet potato chunks in the oil on the prepared baking sheet and season with salt. Roast for 15–20 minutes until soft but still holding their shape. Leave the oven on.

2) Meanwhile, melt the butter in a medium-sized saucepan over a low–medium heat. Add the flour in 2–3 stages, whisking between each addition to combine. Cook for 2 minutes, stirring, then gradually add the milk, a little at a time, whisking constantly to avoid lumps. Once all the milk has been incorporated, bring to a simmer, then stir in the nutmeg and season with salt and pepper.

3) Spoon half the cooked sweet potatoes into the sauce, along with the plant-based cheese, mustard and chipotle paste. Using a stick blender, blend well to combine. (If you don't have a stick blender, transfer the mixture to a blender or food processor.)

4) Meanwhile, bring a large saucepan of well-salted water to the boil and cook the macaroni for 8–10 minutes (or 1 minute less than the packet instructions). Drain in a colander and cool under cold water, draining well once more.

5) Return the drained pasta to the pan, then add the cheese sauce and the remaining roasted sweet potato chunks. Stir well to combine. Spoon the mixture into a baking dish, then top with another handful of grated vegan cheese. Bake for 15–20 minutes until golden.

6) Meanwhile, make the topping. In a food processor, pulse the bread to a large crumb, then add the oil and parsley. Pulse just enough to combine. Stir in the sunflower seeds and nutritional yeast by hand.

7) When the macaroni has cooked, sprinkle over the topping and bake for a further 5 minutes. Remove from the oven and leave to cool for 5–10 minutes before serving.

SERVES 4

500G (1LB 2OZ) SWEET POTATOES, peeled and diced into 1.5–2cm ($^5/_8$–¾in) chunks

1 TABLESPOON VEGETABLE OIL

50G (1¾OZ) PLANT-BASED BUTTER

50G (1¾OZ) PLAIN FLOUR

600ML (20FL OZ) OAT MILK

¼ TEASPOON GROUND NUTMEG

120G (4¼OZ) MATURE CHEDDAR-STYLE VEGAN CHEESE, grated, plus extra for the top

1 TABLESPOON ENGLISH MUSTARD

½ TABLESPOON CHIPOTLE PASTE

200G (7OZ) MACARONI

SALT AND FRESHLY GROUND BLACK PEPPER

For the topping

1 SLICE OF SOFT WHITE BREAD, broken into chunks

½ TABLESPOON OLIVE OIL

1 TABLESPOON CHOPPED FLAT-LEAF PARSLEY

1 TABLESPOON SUNFLOWER SEEDS

1 TEASPOON NUTRITIONAL YEAST

ASPARAGUS & CHICK'N POT PIE

Pies can be quite a lot of work, but this one is so easy you can knock it up in no time. A 'pot pie' is a pie that has a lid but no base. The term originated in England, but this type of pie is particularly popular in America. If asparagus is out of season, then leeks make a great substitute. The creamy filling is perfect with mashed potatoes or boiled new potatoes and minted peas.

1) Preheat the oven to 200°C/180 °C fan/400°F/gas mark 6.

2) Heat 20g (¾oz) of the butter in a large saucepan over a medium heat. Add the chick'n and fry for 5 minutes until golden, then set aside on a plate.

3) Return the pan to the heat and add the remaining butter. Once it has melted, stir in the flour, then cook for 5 minutes. In a jug, whisk the mustard and crumbled stock cube into the oat milk, then gradually add this mixture to the pan, whisking between each addition until smooth. Bring to the boil, then reduce the heat to low and simmer for 3 minutes, stirring constantly, until thickened.

4) Return the chick'n pieces to the pan, along with the asparagus, lemon zest and parsley. Season with the salt and pepper and stir to combine.

5) Spoon the mixture into a 2 litre (3½ pint) ovenproof serving dish. Unroll the puff pastry sheet over the top of dish to cover, trimming if needed. Pinch the edges of the pastry to seal it to the dish. Cut a little cross in the middle of the pie to release steam and prevent the pastry from cracking. (You can cut any trimmings into little leaf shapes to decorate, if you're feeling fancy.)

6) In a small jug or mug, mix the plant-based cream with the maple syrup, then brush the pastry with this mixture. Sprinkle over the thyme leaves, then bake for 25–30 minutes until the pastry is golden and puffed up.

7) Serve the pie with mashed potatoes or steamed new potatoes.

CHEF'S TIP

If you're not a convert to plant-based meat, use chunks of leek instead of the plant-based chick'n.

SERVES 4

120G (4¼OZ) PLANT-BASED BUTTER

350G (12OZ) PLANT-BASED CHICK'N PIECES, cut into 2–3cm (¾–1¼in) chunks

80G (2¾OZ) PLAIN FLOUR

1 TEASPOON WHOLEGRAIN OR DIJON MUSTARD

½ VEGETABLE STOCK CUBE, crumbled

750ML (25FL OZ) OAT MILK

300G (10½OZ) ASPARAGUS, woody ends removed, sliced into 2cm (¾in) chunks

ZEST OF 1 LEMON

1 TABLESPOON FLAT-LEAF PARSLEY, finely chopped

½ TEASPOON SALT

PINCH OF FRESHLY GROUND BLACK PEPPER

1 SHEET OF READY-ROLLED VEGAN PUFF PASTRY

50ML (2FL OZ) PLANT-BASED CREAM

2 TEASPOONS MAPLE SYRUP

GENEROUS PINCH OF THYME LEAVES

MASHED POTATOES (see page 114) or STEAMED NEW POTATOES, to serve

RED LENTIL HARIRA WITH YOGURT

This hearty soup is closer to a stew; rich with tomatoes and lentils and made even more substantial with the addition of vermicelli pasta pieces or, if you prefer, rice. We use a ras el hanout spice mix, which translates as 'top of the shop', implying the finest spices available. Ras el hanout blends vary, but are typically made up of cumin, coriander, cardamom, ginger and saffron. The fragrant spices infuse the soup with aroma, making this comforting bowl the perfect thing to come home to after a long, rainy day.

SERVES 6–8

4–5 TABLESPOONS OLIVE OIL

2 ONIONS, finely diced

2CM (¾IN) PIECE OF FRESH ROOT GINGER, finely chopped

1 TABLESPOON RAS EL HANOUT OR BAHARAT SPICE MIX

½ TEASPOON GROUND TURMERIC

1 TEASPOON CUMIN SEEDS

2 BAY LEAVES

2 CARROTS, peeled and finely diced

2 CELERY STICKS, peeled and finely diced

HANDFUL OF FLAT-LEAF PARSLEY, stalks finely chopped, leaves roughly chopped

100G (3½OZ) RED LENTILS, rinsed well and drained

1.5 LITRES (2½ PINTS) VEGETABLE STOCK

2 TABLESPOONS TOMATO PURÉE

400G (14OZ) TOMATO PASSATA

1–2 TABLESPOONS HARISSA PASTE (rose harissa works really well here), plus extra to decorate (optional)

1 TEASPOON CASTER SUGAR

100G (3½OZ) VERMICELLI PASTA PIECES OR 150G (5½OZ) COOKED RICE

SALT AND FRESHLY GROUND BLACK PEPPER

To serve

COCONUT YOGURT

LEMON WEDGES (optional)

1) Heat the oil in a large, heavy-based saucepan over a medium heat. Add the onions and cook for 2 minutes until translucent and golden, then reduce the heat to low and add the ginger, spices and bay leaves. Cook gently for a few seconds until fragrant. Next, add the carrots, celery and parsley stalks, and cook for another 5 minutes until the carrots are starting to lose their bite.

2) Add the red lentils and cook for 5 minutes, then add the stock, tomato purée, passata, harissa and sugar. Bring to a simmer, then cook gently, stirring often, for 20–30 minutes until the lentils are cooked.

3) Add the vermicelli pasta or rice and cook for a further 5–10 minutes until the pasta is cooked. Season the soup with salt and pepper.

4) Serve topped with the parsley leaves and dollops of coconut yogurt, with extra harissa on top and lemon wedges on the side for squeezing, if you like.

GOMA DARE SOBA

Goma dare, or Japanese sesame dressing, is excellent on salads, stir-fried vegetables or noodles. A small jar of this sauce is a great shortcut for a mid-week meal. This recipe makes about twice as much dressing as you need for the noodles, so keep the rest in the fridge and enjoy another day – it will keep for up to 3 days. We've used soba noodles here because they are made with buckwheat, which gives them a delicious, nutty taste – and also means they are usually gluten-free. They can be served cold, making this a perfect fresh main for a warm day.

SERVES 2

100G (3½OZ) SOBA NOODLES

100G (3½OZ) EDAMAME BEANS, peeled and podded

125G (4½OZ) SUGAR SNAP PEAS, halved lengthways

3 SPRING ONIONS, finely sliced

SPLASH OF SESAME OIL

For the goma dare *sauce*

100G (3½OZ) TAHINI

2 TABLESPOONS SOY SAUCE OR TAMARI

2 TABLESPOONS SESAME OIL

2 TABLESPOONS RICE VINEGAR

2 TABLESPOONS AGAVE SYRUP

1 TABLESPOON VEGAN MAYO (shop-bought, or see our recipe on page 170)

1 TEASPOON MISO PASTE

To serve

PINCH OF SEA SALT

TOASTED SESAME SEEDS OR *FURIKAKE* (RICE SEASONING)

CUCUMBER, julienned

SUSHI GINGER STRIPS

1) Add all the ingredients for the sauce to a small bowl or jar and whisk well to combine. If it looks too thick, you can whisk in a little water.

2) Bring a large saucepan of water to the boil – soba noodles need lots of space. Add the noodles and follow the cooking time on the packet carefully, setting a timer for 30 seconds before the noodles should be finished.

3) When the timer goes off, throw in the edamame beans and sugar snap peas for the final 30 seconds, then drain, cooling immediately with plenty of cold water. Drain well, then tip into a large bowl. Add the spring onions and sesame oil and toss well, then pour over half the *goma dare* sauce (the remainder can be stored in the fridge for up to 3 days) and toss to coat.

4) Serve in a bowl with a pinch of sea salt and some toasted sesame seeds or *furikake*, along with the cucumber and sushi ginger.

CHEF'S TIP

Soba noodles are delicious, but be warned: they must be cooked with care as they can be easily overcooked, and they should be chilled as quickly as possible after cooking to prevent them from sticking together.

SHIITAKE TEMPEH BALLS

Tempeh is great for making meatball-style dishes, as it has a nutty and slightly sticky texture, which means it can be crushed and rolled. The shiitakes used here add such a strong, meaty flavour and texture to the dish. These are great with the Kecap Manis Tenderstem Broccoli with Crushed Peanuts (see page 150) or our Goma Dare Soba (see opposite), but also make a nice, light meal accompanied by a simple salad with cucumber and baby leaves dressed in rice vinegar.

1) Heat 1 tablespoon of the sesame oil in a frying pan over a low–medium heat. Add the shiitake and cook for a couple of minutes until the mushrooms are becoming tender but not drying out.

2) Break apart the tempeh into a mixing bowl. If it is too hard to break apart with your hands, you can grate it on the large side of a box grater. Add the mushrooms, along with the sesame seeds, ginger, salt and chopped coriander, and mix well with your hands to combine. Once you're happy with the texture, shape the mixture into little balls of about 30g (1oz) each.

3) Heat the remaining tablespoon of sesame oil in a frying pan over a low heat (you can use the same pan as before). Add the tempeh balls and fry for 6–8 minutes until cooked through.

4) Drizzle the Kecap Manis sauce over the tempeh balls and serve with your chosen accompaniment.

SERVES 4

2 TABLESPOONS SESAME OIL

300G (10½OZ) SHIITAKE MUSHROOMS, chopped

400G (14OZ) TEMPEH

1 TEASPOON TOASTED SESAME SEEDS

3CM (1¼IN) PIECE OF FRESH ROOT GINGER, peeled and finely grated

1 TEASPOON SALT

1 TABLESPOON FINELY CHOPPED CORIANDER

4 TABLESPOONS KECAP MANIS (see page 150)

YOUR CHOSEN ACCOMPANIMENT, to serve (see recipe intro)

CHEF'S TIP

The shiitake and tempeh mixture can be prepared in advance and stored in the fridge in a sealed container for up to 24 hours.

SEE IMAGE, OVERLEAF

PACCHERI WITH PORCINI CREAM

Paccheri is a cute, short, wide pasta originating in Campania in Southern Italy; it looks a little like cut-up rigatoni. The word means 'hands', and is still used in Italian to describe an open-handed, friendly pat. As the story goes, paccheri pasta was invented to smuggle Italian garlic cloves across borders; they were tucked into the pasta. Look for pasta made from 100 per cent semolina wheat; this means it will retain its shape and firmness when cooked. This recipe uses dried porcini to create a rich and creamy sauce packed with flavour (but please note they need an hour to soak). This is perfect with a glass of red wine.

SERVES 4

30G (1OZ) DRIED PORCINI

300ML (½ PINT) BOILING WATER

400G (14OZ) PACCHERI OR SCHIAFFONI PASTA

80G (2¾OZ) PLANT-BASED BUTTER

½ TABLESPOON EXTRA VIRGIN OLIVE OIL

1 GARLIC CLOVE, finely chopped

PINCH OF DRIED CHILLI FLAKES

1 TABLESPOON CHOPPED THYME LEAVES

300G (10½OZ) CHESTNUT MUSHROOMS, sliced

200ML (7FL OZ) PLANT-BASED CREAM

SALT AND FRESHLY GROUND BLACK PEPPER

To serve

1 TABLESPOON CHOPPED FLAT-LEAF PARSLEY

2 TABLESPOONS CHOPPED TOASTED WALNUTS

1) Place the porcini in a bowl and pour over the boiling water. Leave to soak for about 1 hour, stirring occasionally to make sure the mushrooms are rehydrating evenly. When the porcini are nicely puffed up and tender, drain, reserving the soaking liquor. Chop the porcini into small chunks.

2) Bring a large saucepan of salted water to the boil and add the pasta. Cook for 3 minutes less than instructed on the packet, then drain, reserving the cooking water.

3) Meanwhile, melt the butter in a sauté pan or large non-stick frying pan with the oil over a low–medium heat. Add the garlic, chilli and thyme and cook gently for 2 minutes until fragrant, taking care not to burn the garlic. Add the chestnut mushrooms and chopped porcini and cook for 2 minutes.

4) Add the porcini soaking liquor, then increase the heat to medium–high and cook for 10 minutes to reduce the liquid by about half. Add the cream and season with the salt and pepper to taste. Stir and simmer for 5 minutes more.

5) Remove about half the sauce and transfer it to a blender, along with half a ladleful of the pasta cooking water. Blend until smooth, then return to the pan and stir to combine.

6) Add the drained pasta to the pan with the creamy sauce and stir to combine, then add about 200ml (7fl oz) of the pasta cooking water. Cover with a lid and let the liquid reduce by about half so that the sauce coats the pasta – this should take about 5 minutes. If it starts to become too dry, add another splash of the cooking water.

7) Add the chopped parsley and stir for 1 minute more, then taste and adjust the seasoning if necessary. Sprinkle over the toasted walnuts and serve.

CHEF'S TIP

Fresh porcinis are much tastier than dried, if you can get them, but they have a short season. You can buy them fresh and freeze them for up to 3 months, if you like. You'll need 350g (12oz) fresh porcini to make this dish.

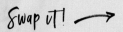 **Swap it!** →

If you can't find long-stemmed large-
leaf spinach, don't use baby spinach
instead; it won't have sufficient
flavour or texture. Chard makes a
great substitute, and can be prepared
and cooked in the same way.

SPINACH & PINE NUT FILO PIE

I love baby spinach for its convenience; it cooks in seconds, is easy to wash and works well in a salad. However, when it comes to flavour, the big stuff has it beat, hands down. I always cook the stems, finding them delicious and tender, with a pleasant texture that enhances fillings for pastries or flatbreads. Bunches of large-leaf spinach tend to be muddy or gritty, so be sure to wash them really well. This filo pie can be assembled in advance and cooked just before your guests arrive, leaving your kitchen spotless and you looking cool as a cucumber.

1) Preheat the oven to 180°C/160°C fan/350°F/gas mark 4 and grease a 20cm (8in) square ovenproof dish with some of the sun-blushed tomato oil.

2) Heat the vegetable or rapeseed oil in a large non-stick frying pan over a medium heat and add the leek(s). Fry for 5 minutes until slightly softened, then add the garlic and chopped spinach stems. Cook for 2–3 minutes, then add the shredded leaves. Increase the heat to medium–high and cook for 2 minutes to wilt the spinach, then take off the heat and tip the mixture into a colander to drain.

3) When cool enough to handle, squeeze the spinach mixture to release any excess liquid, then tip into a large bowl. Add the sun-blushed tomatoes, pine nuts, feta, dill and rice. Stir to combine and season to taste.

4) Using the oil from the tomatoes, brush a layer of the filo and press it into the prepared dish or tray, allowing the sheet to overlap the edges of the dish. Repeat, layering the filo to cover the entire dish, until you have just 1 sheet left, making sure you brush each layer well with the oil. Tip the spinach mixture into the dish or tray and then fold over the edges of the filo sheets. Brush the last filo sheet with oil and fold to fit the top of the dish or tray, then place it on top, covering the filling. Brush the top of the pie with a little more oil, then use a sharp knife to cut the filo down the middle and then the other way, to form a cross. Then cut from corner to corner both ways (until it looks bit like a Union Jack flag).

5) Bake the pie for 30–35 minutes until the pastry is golden and crunchy, then serve with the salad, if you like.

SERVES 4–6

220G (8OZ) JAR SUN-BLUSHED TOMATOES, drained and sliced (retain the oil)

1 TABLESPOON VEGETABLE OR RAPESEED OIL

1 LARGE OR 2 SMALL LEEKS, trimmed and sliced

5 GARLIC CLOVES, grated or finely chopped

400G (14 OZ) LARGE-LEAF SPINACH, washed and drained, stems chopped into 2cm (¾in) slices and leaves shredded

50G (1¾OZ) TOASTED PINE NUTS

75G (2¾OZ) VEGAN FETA-STYLE CHEESE, crumbled

35G (1¼OZ) DILL, chopped

150G (5½OZ) COOKED LONG-GRAIN RICE

10 SHEETS OF FILO PASTRY (about 270g/9½oz)

SALT AND FRESHLY GROUND BLACK PEPPER

SOFT HERB SALAD (see page 145), to serve (optional)

ARTICHOKE FIDEUÀ

This dish is similar to paella, but it is made with fideus, a type of short, chopped, toasted vermicelli pasta. The end result is just as impressive as paella, but much easier to make. *Fideuà* is traditionally made with seafood, but we have used artichoke hearts. If you can't find the Spanish fideus pasta, you can use the chopped vermicelli commonly found in shops with a good Turkish or Middle Eastern section, or capellini spezzati.

This is a one-pot recipe that starts on the stovetop and is finished in the oven. You can tell it's ready when the pasta is standing up, and you have an exquisite crunch on the bottom. In Catalan this is known as *socarrat*, and your guests will be sure to fight over it!

SERVES 4

150G (5½OZ) FIDEUS PASTA, OR BROKEN VERMICELLI OR CAPELLINI SPEZZATI

2–3 TABLESPOONS EXTRA VIRGIN OLIVE OIL

1 LITRE (1¾ PINTS) VEGETABLE STOCK

1 CARROT, peeled and finely diced

1 SMALL RED ONION, diced

1 CELERY STICK, finely diced

1 YELLOW PEPPER, sliced

480G (1LB 1OZ) JAR ARTICHOKE HEARTS IN BRINE, drained and sliced

1 TEASPOON PAPRIKA

BIG PINCH OF SAFFRON

½ TEASPOON SALT

200G (7OZ) FROZEN PEAS

For the herb paste

3 GARLIC CLOVES, chopped

½ TABLESPOON EXTRA VIRGIN OLIVE OIL

20G (¾OZ) FLAT-LEAF PARSLEY, chopped

⅛ TEASPOON SALT

To serve

VEGAN AIOLI (see page 170)

1 LEMON, cut into wedges

1) If you're using vermicelli or capellini spezzati, preheat the oven to 200°C/ 180°C fan/400°F/gas mark 6. Tip the pasta into a baking tray and drizzle over 1 tablespoon of the oil. Toss to coat, then toast the pasta in the oven for 8–10 minutes until deep golden brown, shaking the tray once or twice to ensure even browning. Remove and allow to cool completely. (You can skip this step if you're using fideus pasta.)

2) Increase the oven temperature to 230°C/210°C fan/450°F/gas mark 8.

3) In a medium saucepan over a medium heat, bring the vegetable stock to a simmer.

4) Meanwhile, make the herb paste by placing all the ingredients in a food processor, and blitzing to form a green paste. Alternatively, chop the ingredients, then pound to a paste in a pestle and mortar. Set aside.

5) Heat the remaining 2 tablespoons of oil in a 30cm (12in) ovenproof paella pan, or any wide, shallow frying pan, over a high heat. Add the carrot, onion and celery, and cook for 4 minutes until the onion is translucent. Add the pepper and artichoke hearts, then cook for 2 minutes more.

6) Reduce the heat to low–medium and stir in the pasta, followed by the paprika, green herb paste, saffron and salt. Stir to combine, then add 750ml (25fl oz) of the warm stock to the pan, shaking it to settle and loosen any pasta clusters as the stock begins to boil. Only shake the pan at this stage – do not stir.

7) Simmer for about 10 minutes. Once the pasta no longer has room to swim, add the remaining stock and continue to simmer the fideuà for about 5 minutes until only a thin (almost invisible) layer of stock rests on top.

8) Scatter the peas on top, then transfer the pan to the oven and bake for 12–15 minutes until all the stock has evaporated. The pasta should be standing up, with a crunchy layer or crust on the bottom.

9) When it's ready, spoon the aioli around the fideuà and serve with lemon wedges for squeezing.

LEEK & PINE NUT GNOCCHI GRATIN

A hearty, warming meal, the gnocchi here are baked and topped with a crunchy breadcrumb or *pangratatto* topping, making for a satisfying mix of creaminess and crunch. Ready-made gnocchi have become widely available, and most types are vegan, but check the ingredients just in case.

1) Preheat the oven to 200°C/180°C fan/400°F/ gas mark 6.

2) Place the garlic on a chopping board and crush into a paste with the side of a large knife. Place the parsley on top and finely chop so that the garlic and parsley combine. Set aside.

3) Heat the oil in a large sauté pan or frying pan over a low heat. Add the leeks, cover with a lid and cook for 15 minutes. Once the leeks are soft, remove the lid, increase the heat to high and add the cherry or baby plum tomatoes, water and plant-based cream. Stir well and cook for 10 minutes.

4) In a small bowl or mug, mix the cornflour with a splash of cold water, then add this to the pan. Cook, stirring, for 5 minutes, then season with the lemon zest, salt and pepper. Turn off the heat.

5) Remove half the sauce from the pan and transfer to a blender or food processor. Blend until smooth, then pour back into the pan.

6) Meanwhile, cook the gnocchi in a large pan of salted boiling water according to the packet instructions, making sure they still have bite.

7) Drain the gnocchi and add them to the sauce, along with 50g (1¾oz) of the pine nuts and the chopped parsley and garlic mixture. Add 60g (2¼oz) of the plant-based cheese and stir well.

8) Spoon the mixture into a baking dish and sprinkle the remaining cheese and pine nuts on top.

9) Prepare the *pangrattato* by pulsing the bread to a large crumb in a food processor. Add the oil, parsley and some salt, and pulse just enough to combine well and make green breadcrumbs. Sprinkle these over the top of the gratin.

10) Bake for 15 minutes until bubbling and golden on top. Remove from the oven and allow to sit for 5–10 minutes before serving.

SERVES 4

2 GARLIC CLOVES

30G (1OZ) FLAT-LEAF PARSLEY, leaves picked

2 TABLESPOONS OLIVE OIL

3 LEEKS, trimmed and finely sliced

125G (4½OZ) CHERRY TOMATOES OR BABY PLUM TOMATOES, halved

100ML (3½FL OZ) WATER

250ML (9FL OZ) PLANT-BASED CREAM

1 TEASPOON CORNFLOUR

ZEST OF 2 LEMONS

½ TEASPOON SALT AND A PINCH OF FRESHLY GROUND BLACK PEPPER

600G (1LB 5OZ) VEGAN POTATO GNOCCHI

60G (2OZ) TOASTED PINE NUTS

80G (2¾OZ) MATURE CHEDDAR-STYLE VEGAN CHEESE, grated

For the pangrattato

2 SLICES OF BREAD, torn into pieces

2 TABLESPOONS OLIVE OIL

1 TEASPOON CHOPPED FLAT-LEAF PARSLEY

SALT

SAUSAGE & MUSTARD MASH WITH RED WINE GRAVY

It's important to us that you never feel like you are missing out when eating plant-based food. If you grew up eating delicious sausage and mash, we want to make sure you can still eat delicious sausage and mash. There are tons of great plant-based sausages available; just choose your favourite.

SERVES 4

8 PLANT-BASED SAUSAGES

BLANCHED GREENS OR SAVOY CABBAGE, to serve

For the mashed potatoes

1KG (2LB 4OZ) POTATOES, such as Maris Piper, peeled and cut into large chunks

200ML (7FL OZ) OAT OR SOY MILK

100G (3½OZ) PLANT-BASED BUTTER

PINCH OF GRATED NUTMEG

1 TABLESPOON WHOLEGRAIN MUSTARD

SALT AND FRESHLY GROUND BLACK PEPPER

For the red wine gravy

375ML (12½FL OZ) RED WINE

5 THYME SPRIGS

1 GARLIC CLOVE, sliced

2 TABLESPOONS SOY SAUCE OR TAMARI

2 TABLESPOONS TOMATO PURÉE

300ML (½ PINT) VEGETABLE STOCK

1 TEASPOON TAPIOCA STARCH

1) For the mash, rinse the potato chunks to wash off the excess starch, then tip into a large saucepan filled with plenty of water. Add 1 tablespoon of salt, then place over a medium heat and bring to the boil. Cook for 20 minutes until the potatoes are soft but not falling apart or waterlogged.

2) Meanwhile, in a separate saucepan over a low heat, combine the milk, butter, nutmeg, mustard and 1 teaspoon of salt. Gently cook until the butter has melted.

3) While the potatoes are cooking, cook the sausages according to the packet instructions, and prepare the gravy. Pour the red wine into a saucepan over a low–medium heat. Add the thyme and garlic and cook down until the liquid has almost disappeared. Stir in the soy sauce or tamari and tomato purée and cook for a few more minutes until nice and thick. Add the stock and simmer for 10 minutes to reduce.

4) In a small bowl or mug, mix the tapioca with a splash of water to form a smooth paste. Pour this into the gravy mixture and stir until thickened. Strain through a sieve, then keep the gravy warm while you mash the potatoes.

5) When the potatoes are cooked, drain well and return to the pan, then mash with a potato masher or ricer straight away before they cool.

6) Add the warm butter mixture to the potatoes a little at a time, stirring well with a whisk between each addition. Add only as much as is required to achieve a thick, creamy, fluffy mash. If you need it, you can add a splash more milk.

7) When ready to serve, pile the mash on your plates, then top with the sausages and pour over the gravy. Serve with greens or cabbage.

crowd-pleasers

PEPPER CHICK'N ENCHILADA ROJA

The smell of this *roja* sauce will fill your kitchen. This bright red, mildly spiced sauce can be prepared in advance and will keep for a week in the fridge. It is very simple to make, but does require a specific type of dried chilli: the guajillo. These can be found quite easily – they may not be in your local supermarket, but you'll find them in speciality shops or online, and there really is no beating them for their extraordinary colour and flavour.

SERVES 4

1 RED PEPPER, sliced

1 YELLOW PEPPER, sliced

6 OREGANO SPRIGS, leaves picked

150G (5½OZ) PLANT-BASED CHICK'N, shredded

½ TEASPOON SALT

¼ TEASPOON FRESHLY GROUND BLACK PEPPER

1 TABLESPOON VEGETABLE OIL

10 CORN TORTILLAS

150G (5½OZ) VEGAN CHEDDAR-STYLE CHEESE, grated

For the roja *sauce*

4 DRIED GUAJILLO CHILLIES, tops removed, deseeded

1 DRIED ANCHO CHILLI, top removed, deseeded

¼ TEASPOON OREGANO LEAVES

4 GARLIC CLOVES

250ML (9FL OZ) VEGETABLE STOCK

300G (10½OZ) PASSATA

SALT, TO TASTE

To serve

SHREDDED LETTUCE

FINELY SLICED ONION

SLICED RED CHILLIES

1) To make the *roja* sauce, heat a non-stick frying pan or large, heavy-based saucepan over a high heat and toast the dried chillies for a couple of minutes until fragrant, but do not allow them to burn. Add 1 litre (1¾ pints) of water and bring to a simmer. Continue to simmer for 8–10 minutes until the chillies are rehydrated and soft.

2) Drain the rehydrated chillies then place them in a food processor. Add the oregano, garlic, stock and passata, then season to taste and blend until you have a red, smooth sauce.

3) Combine the red and yellow peppers, oregano and shredded chick'n in a large mixing bowl. Season with the salt and pepper.

4) Preheat the oven to 160°C/140°C fan/325°F/gas mark 3 or preheat your grill to low.

5) Heat the oil in a frying pan over a medium heat. Dip 1 of the tortillas into the roja sauce, making sure it is lightly coated on both sides, then add it to the pan. Fry the tortilla for a few seconds on each side – make sure you do not fry it for too long, or it will become crispy and you won't be able to fold or roll it.

6) To assemble the enchilada, place a spoonful of the chick'n and pepper salad in the centre of the tortilla, then roll it up and place it in a 23 × 33cm (9 × 13in) baking dish. Repeat with the remaining tortillas, *roja* sauce and filling.

7) Once all the enchiladas are rolled, sprinkle with the vegan cheese and grill or bake for 5 minutes to melt the cheese and warm through.

8) Serve the enchiladas immediately while they still are warm, with some shredded lettuce, sliced onion and sliced chillies on top.

FIVE-SPICE TOFU BÁNH MÌ

The secret to this Vietnamese street-food classic is the beautiful contrast in texture and flavour, thanks to the earthy mushroom parfait, spicy carrot pickles, sweet hoisin sauce and crispy tofu. In Vietnam, *bánh mì* carts often offer soft cheese (the foil triangle type) too, so if you don't have the mushroom parfait, you can try switching in vegan cream cheese to add a layer of richness.

1) Begin by preparing the tofu. Drain the tofu well and pat it dry with kitchen paper. Cut into 12 pieces, each about 1.5cm ($^5/_8$in) thick.

2) Place the cornflour, salt and five spice in a mixing bowl and stir together. Coat each piece of tofu well in the spiced flour.

3) Arrange a wire rack over a baking tray so you have somewhere to drain the tofu after frying, then pour oil into a large non-stick frying pan or heavy-based saucepan to a depth of 1cm ($^1/_2$in). Place over a medium–high heat. Heat the oil to 170°C (340°F). If you don't have a cooking thermometer, you can test to see if it's ready by dropping in a small cube of white bread; it should bubble and go golden.

4) Working in batches, carefully add the tofu pieces to the oil and fry for 2–3 minutes on each side until golden brown, turning over carefully when each side is crisp. Set aside on the prepared rack while you fry the rest.

5) To prepare the *bánh mì*, open the baguettes and spread the Mushroom Parfait on the bottom halves and the Gochujang Sesame Mayo on the top halves. Lay the lettuce leaves over the mushroom parfait, then layer on the fried tofu. Drizzle over the hoisin, then finish with the Carrot & Lime Leaf Pickles, coriander, mint and chilli. Close the *bánh mì* and serve.

SERVES 4

1 LARGE CRUSTY BAGUETTE, cut into 4 portions, or 4 SMALL BAGUETTES

6 TABLESPOONS MUSHROOM PARFAIT (see page 28)

4 TABLESPOONS GOCHUJANG SESAME MAYO (see page 171)

8 BABY GEM LETTUCE LEAVES, washed and trimmed (or similar lettuce leaves, such as romaine or cos)

4 TABLESPOONS HOISIN SAUCE

2 HANDFULS OF CARROT & LIME LEAF PICKLES (see page 185)

HANDFUL OF CORIANDER, chopped

SMALL HANDFUL OF MINT

1 RED CHILLI, sliced

For the tofu

300G (10½OZ) FIRM TOFU

80G (2¾OZ) CORNFLOUR

1 TEASPOON SALT

1½ TABLESPOONS CHINESE FIVE SPICE

VEGETABLE OR RAPESEED OIL, for frying

ARAYES

Arayes translates from the Arabic as 'brides'; the origin of the name has been lost, but some say that *arayes* are so called because they would have been sold in little white paper parcels, resembling a bridal gown. They are a popular street-food snack in Lebanon and offer a creative use for shop-bought vegan burger patties and mince. These make an excellent addition to a barbecue spread, especially when served with our creamy Whipped Tahini (see page 176) and Shirazi Salad (see page 142).

SERVES 4

2 PITTAS, halved

For the 'meatballs'

2 BEEF-STYLE VEGAN BURGER PATTIES, broken up, or 230G (8OZ) **SEASONED VEGAN MINCE**

1 TABLESPOON OLIVE OIL, plus extra for drizzling

½ **RED ONION**, finely diced

½ **SMALL BUNCH FLAT-LEAF PARSLEY**, finely chopped

1 TEASPOON GROUND CUMIN

2 TABLESPOONS TOASTED PINE NUTS

4 MINT SPRIGS, leaves picked and chopped

PINCH OF ALEPPO PEPPER (PUL BIBER)

3 GARLIC CLOVES, grated

1 SMALL RED CHILLI, diced

½ **SMALL RED PEPPER**, finely diced

PINCH OF SEA SALT FLAKES

¼ **TEASPOON ZA'ATAR**, plus extra to serve

To serve

WHIPPED TAHINI (see page 176)

SHIRAZI SALAD (see page 142)

LEMON WEDGES, for squeezing

1) In a large mixing bowl, combine the 'meatball' ingredients. Mix well, then divide the mixture into 4 and roll each portion into a ball.

2) Stuff each ball into a pitta half and smooth over the edge. Drizzle a little olive oil over the pittas and rub it in.

3) Heat a griddle pan over a medium heat and grill the pittas for 5 minutes on each side, then place upright on the 'meat' side and grill for another 5 minutes (use tongs to hold them steady if needed).

4) Serve immediately, with Whipped Tahini and Shirazi Salad, lemon wedges for squeezing and a sprinkling of za'atar.

KOREAN-STYLE FRIED CHICK'N BURGER

Even the most hardened meat advocate won't miss the flavour with this fully loaded plant-based burger. Our umami-packed Korean-style glaze is super versatile, as it's also great for stir-fries and as a dip. It will keep for at least two weeks in a clean, sealed container in the fridge.

1) Cook the plant-based chick'n burgers according to the packet instructions.

2) Meanwhile, combine all the ingredients for the fragrant herb and shoot mixture in a bowl, and warm the Korean-style Glaze slightly, either in a saucepan over a low heat or in the microwave.

3) When you're ready to assemble, lightly toast the burger buns and smear both halves with the Gochujang Sesame Mayo. Divide the kimchi between the bottom halves of each bun. Toss the cooked chick'n burgers in the warm glaze to coat, then place on top of the kimchi. Top with the fragrant herb and shoot mix, followed by the top halves of the buns.

4) Serve with a crunchy fresh salad and homemade fries or potato wedges, with more Gochujang Sesame Mayo on the side for dipping.

SERVES 4

4 PLANT-BASED CHICK'N BURGERS

125ML (4FL OZ) KOREAN-STYLE GLAZE (see page 179)

4 VEGAN BURGER BUNS, halved

2 HEAPED TABLESPOONS GOCHUJANG SESAME MAYO (see page 171), plus extra for dipping

250G (9OZ) VEGAN KIMCHI

SALAD AND FRIES OR POTATO WEDGES, to serve

For the fragrant herb and shoot mixture

50G (1¾OZ) BEAN SPROUTS

25G (1OZ) CORIANDER LEAVES

25G (1OZ) THAI BASIL LEAVES

25G (1OZ) PEA SHOOTS

BEETROOT TEMPEH SMASH BURGERS

The term 'smash burger' describes the cooking method of rolling the burger mixture into balls and then smashing them down in a hot frying pan. This results in a thin patty with a delicious crunchy edge. This vegan version of the smash burger is brilliantly simple and packed with protein. We've gone for classic burger toppings here, but they're also great with the same toppings as the Korean-Style Fried Chick'n Burger on page 123.

SERVES 4

2 TABLESPOONS VEGETABLE OIL

4 VEGAN CHEESE SLICES (optional)

4 VEGAN BURGER BUNS, halved

4 TABLESPOONS VEGAN MAYO OR RANCH MAYO (shop-bought, or see our recipes on pages 170 and 171)

2 TOMATOES, sliced

4 TABLESPOONS QUICK PICKLED CUCUMBERS (see page 183) (optional)

1 RED ONION, sliced into 4mm (¼in) slices and separated into rings

2 LARGE HANDFULS OF ICEBERG LETTUCE, shredded

For the smash burger patties

250G (9OZ) TEMPEH, grated on the large side of a box grater

200G (7OZ) BEETROOT, grated on the large side of a box grater

2½ TABLESPOONS SOY SAUCE OR TAMARI

½ TEASPOON AGAVE SYRUP

1½ TEASPOONS VEGAN WORCESTERSHIRE-STYLE SAUCE

½ TEASPOON LIQUID SMOKE

½ TEASPOON GROUND WHITE PEPPER

1 TEASPOON SMOKED PAPRIKA

1 TEASPOON GARLIC POWDER

1 TEASPOON YEAST EXTRACT

70G (2½OZ) TAPIOCA FLOUR OR STARCH

1) Place all the smash burger patty ingredients in a large mixing bowl and mix well to combine. Using clean hands, shape the mixture into 4 balls.

2) Heat the oil in a large frying pan over a high heat until super hot. Carefully place the balls in the pan, spacing them out so each has room to be smashed down. After 30 seconds of searing, use a large, heavy spatula to smash the balls flat until they are less than 1cm (½in) thick. Let them cook for 2–3 minutes, or until the edges start to turn brown, then flip them over and cook for 2–3 minutes on the other side. If you want to make cheeseburgers, put a slice of vegan cheese on top of each patty, then splash the pan with a tiny bit of water and quickly cover with a lid; this will create a steam that will melt the cheese uniformly.

3) Meanwhile, lightly toast the burger buns, then spread the mayo on the bottom halves. Top each half with tomato slices followed by a smash burger, then add the pickles (if using), followed by the red onion rings and lettuce. Spread more mayo on the top halves of the buns and place them on top, then serve.

BRAZILIAN-STYLE LOADED HOT DOGS

Hot dogs are huge in Brazil, both in terms of popularity and size! They are the number-one street food, and are available with all kinds of loaded toppings, but the most common is sweetcorn and thin potato chips called *batata pahla*. If you can't find *batata pahla*, crinkle-cut crisps cut into strips make a good alternative. These hot dogs will really wow at a barbecue, and are just as appealing to kids as to grown-ups. We use a little barbecue sauce to give the sweetcorn salsa a smoky kick.

1) Start by preparing the sweetcorn salsa. Preheat your barbecue to high, or place a griddle pan over a high heat. Rub the corn on the cob with the oil and season with salt and pepper. Grill for 6 minutes, turning to cook on all sides and form some nice char marks, then set aside to cool.

2) As soon as the sweetcorn is cool enough to handle, stand the cob on its end and use a knife to carefully cut off the kernels. Transfer these to a bowl and mix with the other salsa ingredients to combine.

3) When you are ready to eat, lightly oil the hot dogs and cook them on the barbecue or in the same griddle plan as before for 5–8 minutes until cooked with char marks.

4) To assemble, spread the mayo over the hot dog buns, then add some shredded lettuce, followed by the hot dogs. Top with the sweetcorn salsa and *batata pahla* crisps, and enjoy.

SERVES 6

1 TABLESPOON VEGETABLE OIL

6 PLANT-BASED HOT DOGS

4–6 TABLESPOONS VEGAN MAYO (shop-bought, or see our recipe on page 170)

6 VEGAN HOT DOG BUNS, halved

FEW HANDFULS OF BABY GEM OR ROUND LETTUCE, shredded

2 HANDFULS OF *BATATA PAHLA* OR SALTED CRINKLE-CUT CRISPS, cut into strips

---

For the sweetcorn salsa

1 CORN ON THE COB

1 TABLESPOON VEGETABLE OIL

3 ROAST RED PEPPERS, peeled (from a jar is fine, but wash and dry them)

1 GREEN CHILLI, finely diced

½ ONION, finely diced

2 TABLESPOONS BARBECUE SAUCE (shop-bought)

ZEST AND JUICE OF 1 LIME

SALT AND FRESHLY GROUND BLACK PEPPER

POTATO & GREEN CHILLI PARATHA PUFFS

These paratha puffs are a great way to make a meal using leftover potatoes. The many layers in parathas are formed by twisting the buttered dough into a spiral and then rolling it out into a flat circle, which creates a flaky texture similar to that of puff pastry. They are fun to make from scratch, but are also readily available as an uncooked frozen product to finish at home. The trick to working with frozen parathas is not to let them fully defrost, as they become too sticky and difficult to handle. Instead, just take them out of the freezer and lay them out, ready to use. Most are vegan, but double check the packet.

MAKES 4–6

4–6 FROZEN UNCOOKED PARATHAS

280G (10OZ) POTATOES, peeled and boiled

1 GREEN CHILLI, chopped

5 MINT LEAVES

2CM (¾IN) PIECE OF FRESH ROOT GINGER, grated

3 GARLIC CLOVES, grated

¼ TEASPOON AMCHUR OR DRIED MANGO POWDER (optional)

½ TEASPOON GROUND CUMIN

40G (1½OZ) BABY SPINACH, chopped

2 SLICES OF VEGAN SMOKED CHEDDAR-STYLE CHEESE, finely chopped

PINEAPPLE ACHAR (see page 180), or **YOUR FAVOURITE INDIAN PICKLE OR CHUTNEY,** to serve

1) Preheat the oven to 200°C/180°C fan/400°F/ gas mark 6 and line a baking sheet with baking parchment.

2) Arrange the parathas on the prepared tray, spacing them well apart so they don't stick together. Let them sit for 5 minutes until the pastry is just starting to defrost.

3) Meanwhile, place the potatoes in a large mixing bowl and smash with a fork. Add the remaining ingredients (except the achar, pickle or chutney) and combine everything.

4) Spoon about 3 tablespoons of the potato mixture on to each paratha and then fold them in half, sealing the edges with your finger or a fork. Their crescent shape will be similar to empanadas or Cornish pasties.

5) Bake for 18–20 minutes until golden and puffed up. Serve warm with the achar, pickle or chutney.

CHEF'S TIP

This recipe is a good way to use a range of leftover vegetables, such as roasted pumpkin or peas. Simply replace half the cooked potatoes with cooked leftover vegetables in the mixing bowl and smash with the rest of the ingredients.

PERSIAN-STYLE JACKFRUIT & WALNUT WRAPS WITH SOFT HERB SALAD

Iranian cuisine is known for its use of fragrant ingredients such as rose, pomegranate, dried limes, apricots and fresh walnuts. This delicious marinade works well with canned jackfruit, which has almost no taste of its own, and so makes a terrific vehicle for this sweet, aromatic blend of flavours.

1) Preheat the oven to 220°C/200°C fan/ 425°F/gas mark 7.

2) To make the marinade, toast the coriander and cumin seeds in a small dry frying pan over a medium heat for a minute or so until fragrant, then transfer to a food processor. Add all the other marinade ingredients and blend to combine.

3) Combine the jackfruit and onions in a baking tray. Pour over the marinade and toss to coat, then roast for 15 minutes, stirring halfway through to ensure even cooking. Remove from the oven and sprinkle in the walnuts and pomegranate seeds.

4) When you're ready to serve, lightly warm the flatbreads in the oven. Smear a tablespoon of yogurt across the middle of each flatbread, then top with the jackfruit mixture, followed by some of the herb salad. Roll and serve immediately.

SEE IMAGE, OVERLEAF ➞

SERVES 4

250G (9OZ) CANNED JACKFRUIT, drained well

2 RED ONIONS, very finely sliced

60G (2¼OZ) TOASTED WALNUTS, chopped

2 TABLESPOONS POMEGRANATE SEEDS

4 FLATBREADS, ideally lavash- or naan-style

4 TABLESPOONS PLANT-BASED YOGURT (we prefer coconut)

BIG HANDFUL OF SOFT HERB SALAD (see page 145)

For the Persian apricot marinade

1 TEASPOON CORIANDER SEEDS

1 TEASPOON CUMIN SEEDS

3 TABLESPOONS VEGETABLE OIL

1 TABLESPOON APRICOT HARISSA, OR ½ TABLESPOONS HARISSA PASTE AND ½ TABLESPOON FINELY CHOPPED DRIED APRICOT

1 TABLESPOON POMEGRANATE MOLASSES

2 GARLIC CLOVES

1 TABLESPOON SOFT LIGHT BROWN SUGAR

¼ TEASPOON SALT

JUICE OF 1 ORANGE

20G (¾OZ) CORIANDER LEAVES, chopped

PORTOBELLO & CARAMELISED ONION FRENCH DIP ROLLS

Like many culinary favourites, the origin of the French dip is contested. Two different Los Angeles sandwich shops claim to have invented this loaded baguette sandwich served with a side of hot red wine gravy – but whoever came up with it, it's a great idea. We have substituted the original roast beef for meaty slices of portobello mushroom to create this delicious vegan version.

SERVES 4

4 SUB OR BAGUETTE ROLLS

4 TABLESPOONS VEGAN MAYO (shop-bought, or see our recipe on page 170)

2 TABLESPOONS VEGAN DIJON MUSTARD

4 HANDFULS OF QUICK PICKLED CUCUMBERS (see page 183)

400ML (14FL OZ) RED WINE GRAVY (see page 114), warm

For the caramelised onions

2 TABLESPOONS OLIVE OIL

600G (1LB 5OZ) ONIONS, finely sliced

For the portobello mushrooms

40G (1½OZ) PLANT-BASED BUTTER

1 TABLESPOON VEGETABLE OIL

500G (1LB 2OZ) PORTOBELLO MUSHROOMS, sliced

5–7 ROSEMARY SPRIGS, leaves picked and very finely chopped

½ TEASPOON GARLIC POWDER

1 TEASPOON GROUND WHITE PEPPER

1½ TABLESPOONS VEGAN WORCESTERSHIRE-STYLE SAUCE

1½ TABLESPOONS SOY SAUCE OR TAMARI

½ TEASPOON SALT

150ML (¼ PINT) STRONG BLOND BEER

1) For the caramelised onions, heat the oil in a sauté pan or large, heavy-based saucepan over a medium–high heat until it is shimmering. Add the onions and stir to coat with the oil. Let them catch a little and turn a deep golden brown, then reduce the heat to medium–low and keep cooking gently, stirring often, until the onions are glossy and golden. This will take 20–30 minutes, so a little patience is required. Take off the heat and set aside.

2) Meanwhile, prepare the mushrooms. Melt the butter and oil in a non-stick frying pan over a medium–high heat. Add the sliced mushrooms and sauté for a couple of minutes to get some caramelisation, stirring and turning frequently with a spatula. Then add the rosemary, garlic powder, white pepper and sauces. The mushrooms should be glossy and not soggy; increase the heat if necessary, so the liquid reduces and all the flavour goes into the mushrooms. Season with the salt.

3) Remove the mushrooms from the pan and set aside on a plate. Deglaze the pan with the beer, increasing the heat to high and cooking it down until the alcohol has cooked off and the liquid is reduced to a couple of tablespoons. Return the mushrooms to the pan and toss through well to combine.

4) To assemble the sandwiches, lightly toast the rolls, then spread each one with mayo and mustard. Top with the mushrooms, pickled cucumbers and caramelised onions, and serve with warm red wine gravy.

CHEF'S TIP

The caramelised onions can be prepared well in advance; they will keep in a clean jar in the fridge for up to a week.

PAN CON TOMATE
WITH AVOCADO & JALAPEÑOS

Whenever you go out for tapas in Barcelona, *pan con tomate* – or *pa amb tomàquet* in Catalan – is pretty much the first dish brought to the table. It's a very quick recipe, made with only five ingredients – bread, tomatoes, garlic, salt and olive oil – and requires almost no actual cooking. The quality of the tomatoes makes all the difference here; they need to be the ripest and sweetest you can find. The avocado and jalapeño we've included are not traditional, but work really well regardless.

SERVES 6–8

550G (1LB 4OZ) RIPE BEEF TOMATOES

2 TABLESPOONS EXTRA VIRGIN OLIVE OIL, plus extra for drizzling

2 CIABATTA, halved through the middle and then cut into thirds to form 6 thin chunks

1 GARLIC CLOVE, halved

SALT AND FRESHLY GROUND BLACK PEPPER

To serve

2 AVOCADOS, peeled, stoned and sliced

2 TABLESPOONS GREEN JALAPEÑO SLICES

SEA SALT FLAKES

1) Preheat the oven to 180°C/160°C fan/350°F/ gas mark 4.

2) Halve the tomatoes through their equators. Position a box grater inside a large bowl, then carefully rub the cut faces of the tomatoes over the large holes of the grater, using the flattened palm of your hand to move the tomatoes back and forth. The flesh should be grated off, while the skins remain intact in your hand. Discard the skins.

3) Season the tomato pulp with salt and pepper, and stir in the olive oil.

4) Toast the bread in the oven for 3–4 minutes until crunchy, then rub the toasted bread with the halved garlic clove to infuse with flavour.

5) Spoon the tomato pulp on to the bread, then top with the avocado and jalapeño slices. Sprinkle with sea salt and drizzle with olive oil to serve.

CHIPOTLE JACKFRUIT TACO SPREAD

This has become a regular and very popular family meal in our house. Jackfruit is amazing when cooked in this way, as its firm chunks gradually break down to form a rich, tender filling. The tacos are great as they are, but we've added ideas for other recipes you can pair them with to turn this into a real feast, if you so wish.

SERVES 3–4

2 TABLESPOONS VEGETABLE OIL

1 ONION, very finely diced

540G (1LB 3OZ) CANNED JACKFRUIT, drained, rinsed and shredded

ABOUT 500ML (18FL OZ) WATER

1 TABLESPOON VERY FINELY CHOPPED DARK CHOCOLATE

8 SMALL CORN TORTILLAS OR TACO SHELLS

SALT AND FRESHLY GROUND BLACK PEPPER

For the chipotle marinade

1 TEASPOON GROUND CORIANDER

1 TEASPOON GROUND CUMIN

1 TEASPOON SMOKED PAPRIKA

ZEST AND JUICE OF ½ ORANGE

1 TEASPOON CHIPOTLE PASTE

2 TABLESPOONS TOMATO PURÉE

1 TEASPOON MISO PASTE

For the quick pico de gallo

3 RIPE PLUM TOMATOES, cores removed, finely chopped

1 ONION, finely diced

1 JALAPEÑO OR GREEN CHILLI, finely chopped

8–10 CORIANDER SPRIGS, chopped

ZEST AND JUICE OF 1 LIME

½ TABLESPOON AGAVE SYRUP

¼ TEASPOON SALT

For the salad

½ HEAD OF ROMAINE LETTUCE, very finely sliced

4 CORIANDER SPRIGS, sliced

3 TABLESPOONS LIME JUICE

PINCH OF SALT

Optional extras

REFRIED BEANS

WHIPPED AVOCADO CREAM (see page 55)

TOASTED COCONUT RICE (see page 161)

VEGAN SOUR CREAM (see page 29)

CONTINUED OVERLEAF ➚

1) To make the chipotle marinade, combine all the ingredients in a small bowl to make a smooth paste.

2) Heat the oil in a large non-stick frying pan over a medium–high heat. Add the onion and fry for 4 minutes until golden, then add the jackfruit and fry for 3–4 minutes. Add the marinade and cook, adding the water a little at a time as necessary, for 5–8 minutes until the jackfruit is broken down. You may not need all the water.

3) Stir in the chocolate and season to taste.

4) Meanwhile, to make the quick pico de gallo, place all the ingredients in a food processor and pulse a few times to combine. Alternatively, just dice everything very finely and combine in a small bowl.

5) To make the salad, simply combine the ingredients in a bowl and toss together.

6) When you're ready to serve, heat the corn tortillas or taco shells according to the packet instructions, then place them on the table, along with the jackfruit mixture, pico de gallo and salad, and any other elements you've chosen to include, then let everyone assemble their own. It's much more fun that way!

CHERMOULA CAULIFLOWER GALETTE

A simple but beautiful centrepiece, this galette is a great way to celebrate cauliflower. The recipe will work with one medium to large cauliflower, but if you have a couple of different types, that's even better. From purple and golden to the psychedelic romanesco, cauliflowers are available in many beautiful variations, and this zesty Middle Eastern marinade brings out the best in all of them.

1) Preheat the oven to 180°C/160°C fan/350°F/ gas mark 4.

2) To make the chermoula marinade, put all the ingredients except the sugar in a blender or food processor and blend in bursts, then stir in the sugar until it dissolves. If you prefer, you can use a stick blender or do it by hand. Simply chop the herbs, preserved lemon and garlic to a fine, even consistency and combine with the remaining chermoula ingredients to form a chunky paste.

3) Arrange the cauliflower florets on a roasting tray. Pour over the marinade and toss to coat, then roast for 8–10 minutes until starting to go golden.

4) Meanwhile, roll out the pastry on a large piece of baking parchment to form an even circle, 3mm (1/8in) thick, dusting with flour as necessary. Prick the middle of the pastry with a fork a few times.

5) Arrange half of the roasted cauliflower in a circle on the pastry, leaving a border of about 5cm (2in) of pastry around the edges. Sprinkle over the vegan feta, then arrange the rest of the cauliflower on top.

6) Fold up the edges of the pastry around the cauliflower and brush with the plant-based cream.

7) Bake the galette for 25–30 minutes until golden and firm.

8) Garnish the galette with the pistachios and serve.

CHEF'S TIP

There are lots of good-quality ready-made chermoula pastes and dressings available to buy. If you wish to use one of these in place of the homemade marinade to save time, simply loosen it up with a little olive oil.

SERVES 4–6

500G (1LB 2OZ) CAULIFLOWER FLORETS

300G (10½OZ) SHOP-BOUGHT SHORTCRUST PASTRY

PLAIN FLOUR, for dusting

70G (2½OZ) VEGAN FETA-STYLE CHEESE, crumbled

PLANT-BASED CREAM, for brushing

CHOPPED PISTACHIOS, to garnish

For the chermoula marinade

½ BUNCH CORIANDER, chopped

1 TEASPOON FRESHLY CHOPPED OREGANO LEAVES

20G (¾OZ) PRESERVED LEMON, deseeded and roughly chopped

2 GARLIC CLOVES

5½ TABLESPOONS OLIVE OIL

1 TEASPOON SALT

½ TEASPOON GROUND TURMERIC

½ TABLESPOON CASTER SUGAR

sides

SHIRAZI SALAD

A colourful, crunchy chopped salad, *shirazi* is one of the most common side dishes in Iran. The flavours are uncomplicated and fresh, and the dish relies very much on the quality of the produce. It makes a great, fresh pairing for many dishes, and is lovely as part of a spread including hummus and warm flatbread.

SERVES 4–6

3 CUCUMBERS, finely diced

5 PLUM TOMATOES, cored and finely diced

1 RED ONION, finely diced

100G (3½OZ) MINT, leaves picked and very finely sliced

JUICE OF 1 LEMON

100ML (3½FL OZ) EXTRA VIRGIN OLIVE OIL

½ TABLESPOONS SALT

½ TEASPOON FRESHLY GROUND BLACK PEPPER

1) In a salad bowl, combine the cucumbers, tomatoes, onion and mint leaves.

2) Drizzle over the lemon juice and oil, then season with the salt and pepper. Toss to combine and serve immediately.

SOFT HERB SALAD

This is a super-simple yet versatile salad that sits well alongside a variety of dishes. It never overpowers, instead acting as a palate cleanser. It makes a great filling for wraps or sandwiches, and is also wonderful alongside heavier dishes like our Arayes on page 122.

1) In a salad bowl, combine the coriander, mint, dill, cucumber, pomegranate seeds and radishes.

2) Season the salad with the lemon juice and salt and toss to combine.

SERVES 2

30G (1OZ) CORIANDER, roughly chopped

15G (½OZ) MINT, leaves picked

30G (1OZ) DILL, leaves picked

1 LARGE CUCUMBER, halved and sliced

100G (3½OZ) POMEGRANATE SEEDS

3 RADISHES, sliced

JUICE OF 1 LEMON

½ TEASPOON SALT

SIMPLE IS BEST POTATO SALAD

The trick with potato salad is to slightly overcook the boiled potatoes. This makes their soft edges dissolve into the mayonnaise, giving the whole thing a wonderfully creamy texture. Potato salad is one of those recipes where the more you mess about with it, the worse it gets. Just make it fresh and serve it straight away – it's never quite as good when it's been sitting in the fridge.

SERVES 4–6

1KG (2LB 4OZ) RED-SKINNED POTATOES, peeled and cut into 2cm (¾in) chunks

1 TABLESPOON SALT

150G (5½OZ) VEGAN MAYO (shop-bought, or see our recipe on page 170)

1 TABLESPOON WHOLEGRAIN MUSTARD

1 TEASPOON SEA SALT FLAKES

5 SPRING ONIONS, finely sliced

3 TABLESPOONS FINELY CHOPPED CHIVES

1) Place the potato chunks in a large saucepan and fill with water. Add the salt and place over a medium–high heat. Bring to a simmer, then simmer for 10–12 minutes, until the potatoes are soft but still holding their shapes.

2) Drain the potatoes well and leave to cool to just above room temperature.

3) Tip the cooled potatoes into a large bowl. Add the mayonnaise, mustard, sea salt flakes, spring onions and chives. Toss to combine and serve straight away.

ACHAR ROAST VEGETABLES

Indian pickles, or *achar*, are preserved in oil, and each type has a unique masala or spice mix. This makes them a fantastic quick-fix marinade for roasted vegetables. They can be served as a side dish to the Hispi Cashew Moilee (see page 89), but they also make a nice light meal in their own right, especially when served with fresh herbs and a little Mango Pickle Yogurt.

1) Preheat the oven to 200°C/180°C fan/400°F/ gas mark 6 and line a baking tray with baking parchment.

2) In a large bowl, combine the achar marinade ingredients. Add the vegetables and toss to coat. then transfer to the prepared baking tray. Roast for 35–40 minutes, turning halfway, until golden and well roasted. Scatter over the coriander leaves and serve with Mango Pickle Yogurt.

SERVES 4

½ **HEAD OF CAULIFLOWER (ABOUT 200G/7OZ)**, broken into florets

1 **SMALL SWEET POTATO**, peeled and cut into thin wedges

½ **AUBERGINE**, cut into wedges

1 **RED PEPPER**, cut into large chunks

10 **CORIANDER SPRIGS**, leaves picked

MANGO PICKLE YOGURT (see page 182), to serve

For the achar *marinade*

3 **TABLESPOONS HOT MANGO PICKLE**

2 **TABLESPOONS RAPESEED OIL**

1 **TEASPOON METHI LEAVES**

10 **FRESH CURRY LEAVES**

1 **TABLESPOON AGAVE SYRUP**

SALT, to taste

SEE IMAGE, OVERLEAF →

KECAP MANIS TENDERSTEM BROCCOLI WITH CRUSHED PEANUTS

Kecap manis (or ketjap manis) is a popular sweet soy sauce from Indonesia. It's not that common, but if you can find it ready-made, then simply skip that part of the recipe below. It's a great condiment and makes a brilliant dressing for simple stir-fried vegetables, like this Tenderstem broccoli. This recipe also works well for purple sprouting broccoli when it's in season.

SERVES 4

2 TABLESPOONS SESAME OIL

400G (14OZ) TENDERSTEM BROCCOLI

½ TEASPOONS CHILLI FLAKES

CRUSHED ROASTED PEANUTS, to serve

For the kecap manis (makes 200ml/7fl oz)

100ML (3½FL OZ) DARK SOY SAUCE

125G (4½OZ) SOFT LIGHT BROWN SUGAR

2 STAR ANISE

1) To make the kecap manis, pour the soy sauce into a small saucepan. Add the sugar and whisk to combine. Place over a low–medium heat and bring to the boil, then add the star anise. Simmer for 10 minutes until the sauce is glossy and thick. Leave to cool, then remove the star anise. The sauce will keep in a sealed container in the fridge for up to a month.

2) To prepare the broccoli, heat the sesame oil in a large non-stick frying pan or wok over a high heat. Add the broccoli and chilli flakes, along with a tiny splash of water, and sauté for 2 minutes.

3) Transfer to a serving dish and drizzle over 2 tablespoons of the kecap manis. Top with the crushed peanuts and serve.

HARISSA PATATAS BRAVAS

This is our Middle Eastern-influenced take on the classic Spanish spicy potato side. These potatoes have been a massive success on our menu. As well as making a great side dish, they're perfect served as a snack while having drinks.

SERVES 4–6

1KG (2LB 4OZ) RED-SKINNED POTATOES, peeled and cut into 2–3cm (¾–1¼in) cubes

2–3 TABLESPOONS HARISSA PASTE

2–3 TABLESPOONS VEGAN AIOLI (see page 170)

SALT

FRONDS FROM 5 DILL SPRIGS, to serve

For the herb oil

10G (¼OZ) ROSEMARY LEAVES

10G (¼OZ) OREGANO LEAVES

2 GARLIC CLOVES, sliced

1 TEASPOON CORIANDER SEEDS

1 TEASPOON CUMIN SEEDS

1 TEASPOON SALT

200ML (7FL OZ) VEGETABLE OR RAPESEED OIL

1) Preheat the oven to 200°C/180°C fan/400°F/ gas mark 6.

2) Prepare the herb oil by combining the ingredients in a blender and blending to form a chunky dressing. Alternatively, finely chop the herbs and garlic, slightly crush the whole spices, and simply stir everything together with the salt and oil.

3) Put the potatoes into a large saucepan and fill with salted water. Place over a high heat and bring to the boil, then reduce the heat to low–medium and simmer for 5 minutes to parboil (they should still be raw in the middle).

4) Drain the potatoes very well, then return to the pan. Pour over the herb oil and toss to coat.

5) Arrange the potatoes in a single layer on a non-stick baking tray, giving them plenty of room so they don't touch each other. (You may need 2 trays.)

6) Roast for 20–25 minutes, turning halfway through, until the potatoes are crisp and golden.

7) Tip the roasted potatoes into a serving dish and drizzle over the harissa paste. Toss to coat, then drizzle over the vegan aioli, scatter over the dill fronds and serve.

SAFFRON ROASTIES

I don't believe there is any better food than a well-prepared roast potato. The saffron adds a little splash of luxury to this otherwise humble but treasured side dish.

1) Preheat the oven to 200°C/180°C fan/400°F/gas mark 6.

2) Place the potatoes in a large saucepan with 1.5 litres (2½ pints) of water. Add the salt and saffron. Place over a medium–high heat and bring to a simmer. Simmer for 10 minutes until the outsides of the potatoes are soft.

3) Meanwhile, pour the oil into a large oven tray (ideally non-stick) and place in the oven to heat.

4) Smash the garlic bulb with a rolling pin and remove any loose, papery skin, but leave the thick skin around the cloves.

5) After the potatoes have cooked for 10 minutes, drain them using a fine sieve so you don't lose the saffron. Return the drained potatoes to the saucepan, then cover with the lid and give it a good, firm shake. The potatoes may fall apart, but don't worry. Drizzle a little oil on to the potatoes, then add the oregano and smashed garlic. Mix gently with a wooden spoon to combine the elements.

6) Remove the hot tray of oil from the oven and carefully scoop the potatoes, garlic and oregano on to the tray, leaving space around each potato chunk (this is very important as it helps them to cook uniformly). Even if some of the chunks have basically turned to mash, don't worry; just scoop them on.

7) Roast the potato mixture for 35–40 minutes, turning over halfway, until the outsides are golden and crunchy. Serve immediately.

SERVES 4–6

1KG (2LB 4OZ) POTATOES, peeled and cut into 4cm (1½in) chunks

1½ HEAPED TABLESPOONS SALT

BIG PINCH OF SAFFRON

200ML (7FL OZ) OIL, plus extra for drizzling

1 GARLIC BULB

5 OREGANO SPRIGS, leaves only

SMASHED CUCUMBERS

Refreshing, sweet and with as little or as much heat as you like, smashed cucumbers make a perfect side for our Goma Dare Soba (see page 102) or Chilli Miso Butter Udon (see page 94). The classic Chinese technique of bashing the cucumber breaks up the centre, forming crunchy cracks that soak up all the flavour from the chilli and garlic. We use a mild but flavourful Chinese chilli oil for this, like black bean chilli oil or crispy chilli oil.

SERVES 4

1 LARGE OR 2 MEDIUM CUCUMBERS

HANDFUL OF CORIANDER LEAVES, chopped

1 TEASPOON TOASTED SESAME SEEDS, to serve

SALT

For the dressing

½ TEASPOON SALT

1½ GARLIC CLOVES, grated

1 TEASPOON CASTER SUGAR

1 TABLESPOON SOY SAUCE OR TAMARI

2 TABLESPOONS RICE VINEGAR

1 TABLESPOON CHINESE CHILLI OIL, or to taste

¼ TEASPOON SICHUAN PEPPERCORNS, ground in a pestle and mortar

1) In a mixing bowl, combine the dressing ingredients. Stir well until the sugar and salt have dissolved, then set aside.

2) On a chopping board, lay a large knife flat against the cucumber(s), and smash it lightly with your other hand. The cucumber(s) should crack open. Chop it into bite-sized pieces, slicing at a 45-degree angle.

3) Tip the cucumber chunks into a large bowl and sprinkle over a pinch of salt. Leave to rest for 10 minutes, then drain any excess liquid from the bowl (this step is optional).

4) Add the cucumber chunks to the dressing in the mixing bowl, then scatter over the coriander. Toss to combine, then transfer to a serving dish and garnish with sesame seeds to serve.

BUTTERMILK RANCH SLAW

The swede adds an element of surprise to this slaw, as it's not an ingredient we usually associate with salad. However, its crunch and mild sweetness work really well in this colourful side. It's also great in burgers.

SERVES 4

300G (10½OZ) SWEDE, peeled and julienned

170G (5¾OZ) CARROTS, peeled and julienned

1 SMALL RED ONION, finely diced

150G (5½OZ) SMALL RED CABBAGE, finely shredded

150G (5½OZ) SMALL WHITE CABBAGE, finely shredded

20G (¾OZ) CHIVES, finely chopped

3 HEAPED TABLESPOONS RANCH MAYO (see page 171)

SPLASH OF CIDER VINEGAR

SALT AND FRESHLY GROUND BLACK PEPPER

1) In a large bowl, mix all the vegetables together, then add the chives. You can keep this mixture in the fridge for up to 3 days before dressing.

2) Dress with the ranch mayo and a splash of cider vinegar, and toss well to coat. Season with salt and pepper to taste and serve.

CHEF'S TIP

If you a have mandoline, this is the perfect time to use it!

MAPLE & MUSTARD PARSNIPS

These parsnips make a lovely autumnal pairing for hearty dishes like our Asparagus & Chick'n Pot Pie (see page 99). I could also happily eat these alone with a handful of peppery rocket leaves to offset the sweetness.

SERVES 4

3 TABLESPOONS RAPESEED OIL

1 TEASPOON SEA SALT FLAKES

1 TABLESPOON WHOLEGRAIN MUSTARD

2 TABLESPOONS MAPLE SYRUP

4 PARSNIPS, peeled and cut into long wedges

1) Preheat the oven to 200°C/180°C fan/400°F/ gas mark 6 and line a baking tray with baking parchment.

2) In a large bowl, combine the oil, sea salt flakes, mustard and maple syrup. Add the parsnips and toss to coat in the mustard mixture.

3) Arrange the parsnips on the prepared baking tray and roast for 35–40 minutes, turning halfway, until they are glossy and golden.

LEMON CASHEW RICE

This long-grain rice with lemon and cashew is the perfect match for our Pepper Chick'n Enchilada Roja (see page 118) or the Chipotle Jackfruit Tacos (see page 135), as its fresh citrus flavour refreshingly cuts through the spices. The richness of the cashew nuts complements the tartness of the lemon.

1) Preheat the oven 170°C/150°C fan/340°F/ gas mark 3½ and line a baking tray with baking parchment.

2) Wash the rice well at least three times until the water runs clear. Drain thoroughly.

3) Heat the oil in a large sauté pan or large heavy-based saucepan over a high heat. Add the rice and fry for about 5 minutes, stirring constantly with a wooden spoon to prevent it from burning, until the rice turns a very light golden colour.

4) Add the turmeric and oregano, then pour in the water. Add the salt, cover with a lid and reduce the heat to low–medium. Cook for 10 minutes, or until the water has been absorbed and the rice feels just past al dente.

5) Meanwhile, prepare the toasted lemon cashews. In a bowl, mix the cashew nuts with the rest of the ingredients, then tip on to the prepared baking tray. Spread them out in a single layer, then roast in the oven for 20 minutes until golden brown. Remove and allow to cool completely before use.

6) When the rice is ready, remove from the heat. Stir in the lemon zest and juice, then cover once more and leave for another 5 minutes to finish steaming in the residual heat.

7) When you're ready to serve, fluff up the rice with a fork and serve with the toasted lemon cashews on top.

SERVES 4

300G (10½OZ) LONG-GRAIN RICE

1 TABLESPOON VEGETABLE OIL

¼ TEASPOON GROUND TURMERIC

¼ TEASPOON DRIED OREGANO

600ML (20FL OZ) WATER

½ TEASPOON SALT

ZEST OF 2 LEMONS AND JUICE OF ½

For the toasted lemon cashews

150G (5½OZ) CASHEW NUTS

JUICE OF ½ LEMON

½ TABLESPOON AGAVE SYRUP

½ TEASPOON DRIED CHILLI FLAKES

½ TEASPOON SEA SALT FLAKES

TOASTED COCONUT RICE

This creamy spiced pilaf is super versatile; we like to pair it with the Hispi Cashew Moilee on page 89. Cooking rice infused with coconut will make your kitchen smell like heaven. Use a good-quality basmati and wash it well – and never uncover or stir the rice as it cooks.

1) Place the rice in a sieve in a bowl. Place under cold running water, swishing the rice with your hand to release excess starch. Keep tipping out the starchy water from the bowl until the water runs clear; this will take up to 10 minutes.

2) Heat the oil in a medium saucepan over a medium–high heat. Add the curry leaves and mustard seeds (if using). Toast for a few seconds until fragrant, then add the rice and toast for 2 minutes. Add the chillies, salt, coconut milk and water, then cover with the lid. Leave to cook for 10–12 minutes until all the liquid is absorbed, then turn off the heat and leave to steam, still covered, for another 2–3 minutes.

3) This is delicious warm or cold (see Chef's Tip, below), garnished with toasted coconut flakes.

SERVES 6

400G (14OZ) BASMATI RICE

2 TABLESPOONS RAPESEED OIL

10 FRESH CURRY LEAVES

¼ TEASPOON BLACK MUSTARD SEEDS (optional)

2 WHOLE DRIED KASHMIRI CHILLIES

½ TEASPOON SALT

400ML (14FL OZ) CAN COCONUT MILK

400ML (14FL OZ) WATER

TOASTED COCONUT FLAKES, to garnish

CHEF'S TIP

If you want to serve this cold, please note that rice needs to be cooled within a maximum of 90 minutes for food safety. You can chill rice more quickly by dividing it into smaller portions, spreading it out on a clean, shallow tray, or putting a container of hot rice into a larger container of cold water or ice. It is dangerous to leave the rice to cool down in the pan as it won't cool rapidly enough.

ZA'ATAR PITTA CHIPS

Za'atar is a type of dried wild thyme that is prized in the Middle East and North Africa. It is most often found in mixes with other spices and sesame seeds. These pitta chips go well with all the hummus recipes in this book (see pages 44–6) as well as the Whipped Feta on page 61 and the Green Tahini Dressing on page 174, but they also make a nice little snack on their own.

SERVES 4

150ML (¼ PINT) OLIVE OIL

1 TEASPOON GARLIC POWDER

2 TABLESPOONS ZA'ATAR, plus extra to serve

1 TEASPOON SEA SALT FLAKES

½ TEASPOON FRESHLY GROUND BLACK PEPPER

3–4 PITTAS, halved and then cut into tortilla chip-sized triangles

1) Preheat the oven to 190°C/170°C fan/375°F/ gas mark 5 and line 2 baking sheets with baking parchment.

2) In a large mixing bowl, combine the oil with the spices and seasoning. Add the pitta triangles and toss to coat, then tip on to the prepared baking sheets, spreading them out so they crisp up well.

3) Bake for 8–10 minutes, stirring halfway, until crisp and golden (some thicker styles of pitta may take up to 15 minutes). If not serving straight away, cool and store in a sealed container – they will keep for up to 3 days.

dressings & pickles

BEETS & NEEPS PICKLES

These bright pink pickles are inspired by the classic turnip pickles popular in the Middle East. They are quick to make and bring a splash of colour to any sharing spread or salad.

MAKES 1 LITRE (1¾ PINTS)

200ML (7FL OZ) CIDER VINEGAR

150ML (5½FL OZ) WATER

100ML (3½FL OZ) AGAVE SYRUP OR 75G (2¾OZ) CASTER SUGAR

½ TEASPOON SALT

4 BAY LEAVES

1 TEASPOON BLACK PEPPERCORNS

2 BEETROOT (AROUND 400G/14OZ), peeled and cut into long thin wedges approximately 1.5cm (⅝in) thick

2 TURNIPS (AROUND 400G/14OZ), peeled and cut into long, thin wedges approximately 1.5cm (⅝in) thick

1) In a large saucepan over a medium–high heat, combine the vinegar, water, agave or sugar, salt, bay leaves and peppercorns. Bring to a simmer and cook for 2–3 minutes, then add the beetroot and turnips and cook for a further 2 minutes.

2) Take off the heat and transfer the contents of the saucepan to a sterilised jar (see Chef's Tip, below). Seal the jar and let the pickles settle overnight at room temperature before storing in the fridge. They'll be ready to eat after 1 week, and will keep for up to a month.

___

CHEF'S TIP

To sterilise jars, place them in a large saucepan and fill with enough water to cover and fill all of the jars. Bring to the boil and boil for 10 minutes.

QUICK AMBA

Amba is a fermented mango condiment popular in Israel and inspired by the food of India. It traditionally uses slowly fermented unripe green mangos, but we have developed our own very tasty – and very quick – amba recipe. Due to its smooth consistency and tangy flavour, amba is a very useful marinade, as in the case of our Amba Chick'n Kebabs (see page 72), but it also makes a great dip, especially when used to top hummus.

1) Heat the oil in a large saucepan over a low heat. Add the spices and cook for 2 minutes to gently temper (don't allow them to burn). Add the mango purée and pickle, water, onion, chilli, salt, ginger and garlic. Increase the heat to high and bring to the boil, then reduce the heat to low–medium and simmer, stirring occasionally, for about 20 minutes until the mango and onion have softened and the liquid has reduced slightly.

2) Remove from the heat and allow to cool slightly, then blend until smooth, either with a stick blender or in a food processor.

3) Use immediately once cool, or store in a sterilised sealed jar or container (see page 166) for up to 1 week in the fridge.

MAKES 600ML (20FL OZ)

1 TABLESPOON VEGETABLE OIL

1 TEASPOON FENUGREEK LEAVES (METHI LEAVES)

½ TEASPOON GROUND TURMERIC

¼ TEASPOON YELLOW MUSTARD SEEDS

1 TEASPOON CUMIN SEEDS

500ML (18FL OZ) MANGO PURÉE

50G (1¾OZ) MANGO PICKLE

100ML (3½FL OZ) WATER

½ ONION, diced

1 GREEN CHILLI, chopped

1 TABLESPOON SALT

1 TEASPOON GRATED GINGER

2 GARLIC CLOVES, finely chopped or grated

VEGAN MAYONNAISE

Vegan mayo is one of the most fun recipes to show people because it's so easy – much easier than conventional mayonnaise – and it is quite magical to watch it come together. The mayo variations we've given here can either be made using the vegan mayo base recipe below, or added to shop-bought vegan mayo. Soy milks can vary, so if your mayo comes out too thin, add a little more oil; if it's too thick, add a little more soy milk until you achieve the desired thick, creamy consistency.

VEGAN MAYO

The addition of the cold-pressed rapeseed oil gives the mayo that classic eggy colour without an overwhelming flavour.

MAKES 400G (14OZ)

150ML (5½FL OZ) UNSWEETENED SOY MILK

1 TABLESPOON DIJON MUSTARD

1 TABLESPOON LEMON JUICE

250ML (9FL OZ) VEGETABLE OR RAPESEED OIL

½ TEASPOON SALT

PINCH OF *KALA NAMAK* (black salt)

2 TABLESPOONS COLD-PRESSED RAPESEED OIL OR EXTRA VIRGIN OLIVE OIL

1) Combine the ingredients in a jug and blend with a stick blender for about 5 minutes until they come together to form a smooth, emulsified mayonnaise. This mayo will keep for 5 days in an airtight container in the fridge.

VEGAN AIOLI

This is our classic garlic mayonnaise recipe and it's so easy to make.

MAKES 400G (14OZ)

400G (14OZ) VEGAN MAYO (shop-bought or homemade, see left)

2 GARLIC CLOVES, finely grated or crushed

1 TABLESPOON COLD-PRESSED RAPESEED OIL

1) Combine the ingredients in a bowl and blend with a stick blender until smooth. This will keep for 5 days in an airtight container in the fridge.

GOCHUJANG SESAME MAYO

We use this toasted sesame and chilli miso mayonnaise for our Korean-Style Fried Chick'n Burgers (see page 123) and to serve with our Kimchi Grilled Cheeze toastie (see page 35).

MAKES 400G (14OZ)

400G (14OZ) VEGAN MAYO (shop-bought or homemade, see opposite)

½ TABLESPOON GOCHUJANG

1 TABLESPOON SESAME OIL

1 TABLESPOON LIME JUICE

To garnish

BLACK AND WHITE SESAME SEEDS, toasted

CAYENNE PEPPER

1) Combine the ingredients in a bowl and blend with a stick blender until smooth.

2) Garnish with the toasted black and white sesame seeds and a sprinkling of cayenne pepper. This will keep for 5 days in an airtight container in the fridge.

RANCH MAYO

This is our version of the classic American buttermilk dressing. We use coconut yogurt to mimic the flavour of the fermented milk.

MAKES 400G (14OZ)

400G (14OZ) VEGAN MAYO (shop-bought or homemade, see opposite)

1 TABLESPOON LEMON JUICE

1 TABLESPOON NUTRITIONAL YEAST

½ TABLESPOON VEGAN DIJON MUSTARD

50G (1¾OZ) COCONUT YOGURT

1 TEASPOON CHIVES, finely chopped

1) Place all the ingredients in a bowl and whisk to combine. This will keep for 3 days in an airtight container in the fridge.

SEE IMAGE, OVERLEAF →

vegan mayo →

ranch mayo →

gochujang sesame mayo

vegan aioli

GREEN TAHINI DRESSING

The creaminess of this dressing combined with its bright green colour makes it great not just for salads but also drizzled over grilled or roasted vegetables. You can even serve it as a dip with warm bread.

MAKES 300ML (½ PINT)

15 FLAT-LEAF PARSLEY SPRIGS

15 CORIANDER SPRIGS

5 DILL SPRIGS

100G (3½OZ) TAHINI

1 TABLESPOON LEMON JUICE

½ TEASPOON SALT

3 TABLESPOONS OLIVE OIL

1 TABLESPOON LIGHT AGAVE SYRUP

¼ TEASPOONS CUMIN SEEDS, toasted and crushed, or ⅛ teaspoon ground cumin

1) Bring a medium saucepan of water to the boil and drop in the herbs. Take off the heat and strain into a colander immediately. Cool the herbs quickly by plunging into ice-cold water, then squeeze to remove excess liquid and roughly chop.

2) Add the herbs to a blender along with the tahini, lemon juice, salt, oil, agave and cumin, and blend until completely smooth. You may need to add a splash of water, as different types of tahini vary in terms of consistency. You are aiming for a bright green colour and a consistency like that of double cream.

3) This will keep in a sealed dressing bottle or jar in the fridge for up to 3 days.

WHIPPED TAHINI

Whipping tahini using this method results in an almost dessert-like thick cream, which is great as a dip for warm bread or grilled pitta, but also makes a useful condiment. We serve this with our Amba Chick'n Kebabs (see page 72).

MAKES 150G (5½OZ)

100G (3½OZ) TAHINI

1 TABLESPOON LEMON JUICE

¼ TEASPOON SALT

¼ TEASPOON CUMIN SEEDS, toasted and crushed, or ⅛ teaspoon ground cumin

2 TABLESPOONS OLIVE OIL

1 TABLESPOON AGAVE OR MAPLE SYRUP

ABOUT 100ML (3½FL OZ) WATER, slightly warm

1) Combine the tahini, lemon juice, salt, cumin, oil and agave or maple syrup in a bowl. Beat with a spoon or electric whisk (or use the paddle attachment on your stand mixer), and gradually add the water, still beating, until the mixture is fluffy and has the texture of half-whipped cream. You may not need all the water if the mixture is starting to look too thin. If it is too thick, you can add a bit more.

2) This will keep in a sealed container in the fridge for up to 5 days.

ROCKET & HAZELNUT PESTO

Pesto roughly translates as 'to pound or crush', so we've given you two different methods to make this version of the classic Italian sauce. This punchy, peppery style of pesto is lovely in a focaccia sandwich with tomatoes, or as a sauce for pasta, as in our Pasta Crudaiola (see page 84).

1) To make this pesto in a food processor, pour 2 tablespoons of the oil over the blades, then add the rocket, hazelnuts, nutritional yeast, salt and garlic. Pulse to combine, while drizzling another 2 tablespoons of the oil into the processor.

2) To make this using a pestle and mortar, combine the nuts, salt and garlic in the mortar and grind with the pestle until smooth, then add 4 tablespoons of the oil very slowly and grind again until smooth. Finely chop the rocket and add it to the mortar, then grind with the other ingredients until a textured paste is formed.

3) Transfer the pesto to an airtight container or jar. Drizzle the remaining oil over the top to cover. This will keep in the fridge for up to 3 days.

MAKES 120G (4¼OZ)

6 TABLESPOONS EXTRA VIRGIN OLIVE OIL

60G (2¼OZ) ROCKET

80G (2¾OZ) HAZELNUTS, roasted, skinned and chopped

2 TEASPOONS NUTRITIONAL YEAST

⅛ TEASPOON SALT

1 GARLIC CLOVE

CHEF'S TIP

To keep the vibrant green colour, add an ice cube to the food processor while you pulse.

The quality of the pesto is dependent on the individual ingredients, and the strength of the ingredients depends on the season or variety, so taste it as you go, and adjust the quantities as needed.

KOREAN-STYLE GLAZE

A rich, sweet marinade with gentle spice from the gochujang paste, this glaze is the key to our best-selling Korean-Style Fried Chick'n Burger (see page 123). It is also a useful dip or stir-fry sauce (see our recipe for Bokkeumbap on page 96).

1) In a saucepan, combine the garlic, ginger, soy sauce or tamari, gochujang, sugar, vinegar and 5 tablespoons of the water, and heat gently over a low heat for 5–10 minutes, stirring frequently, until the sugar has dissolved.

2) In a small bowl, combine the cornflour with the remaining 2 tablespoons of water to form a smooth paste. Add the cornflour paste to the saucepan and slightly raise the temperature. Continue to stir for 2–3 minutes until the sauce becomes thick and glossy.

3) Take off the heat and allow to cool, then whisk in the sesame oil and sesame seeds. Transfer to a sterilised bottle or jar (see page 166) and store in the fridge for up to 2 weeks.

MAKES 380G (13OZ)

2 GARLIC CLOVES, minced or finely grated

2CM (¾IN) PIECE OF FRESH ROOT GINGER, peeled and finely grated

120ML (4FL OZ) SOY SAUCE OR TAMARI

120G (4¼OZ) GOCHUJANG

120G (4¼OZ) SOFT LIGHT BROWN SUGAR

1 TABLESPOON RICE VINEGAR

7 TABLESPOONS WATER

1 TABLESPOON CORNFLOUR

1 TABLESPOON SESAME OIL

1 TABLESPOON SESAME SEEDS

PINEAPPLE ACHAR

We love this achar, which we serve alongside our Sri Lankan *kiri hodi* (coconut milk curry). It's salty, sour and sweet all at once, and pairs really well with creamy flavours.

MAKES 500G (1LB 2OZ)

1 PINEAPPLE, peeled, spines removed and flesh cut into small chunks, or **500G (1LB 2OZ) PREPPED PINEAPPLE CHUNKS**, halved

½ TEASPOON GROUND TURMERIC

1 TEASPOON CORIANDER SEEDS

1 TEASPOON DRIED FENUGREEK LEAVES (METHI)

2 TABLESPOONS KASHMIRI CHILLI POWDER

1 TABLESPOON DRIED CHILLI FLAKES

½ TABLESPOON SALT

JUICE OF 1 LEMON

1 TEASPOON SOFT DARK BROWN SUGAR

300ML (½ PINT) RAPESEED OIL

1) In a large bowl place, combine the pineapple chunks with all the spices and the salt. Using a wooden spoon, mix very well so that the spices uniformly coat the pineapple pieces. Taste to check the seasoning; it should be slightly salty. If not, then add more salt.

2) Add the lemon juice and sugar and stir again.

3) Heat the oil in a large pan over a medium–low heat. You want to heat it just enough to make it hot, then let it cool to room temperature. Once cool, add it to the bowl with the pineapple and stir to combine.

4) Transfer the achar to a large, sterilised jar (see page 166), pressing down the pineapple with a spoon to ensure all of it is submerged in the oil. Cover with an airtight lid. This will be ready to use after 2 days, and will keep in the fridge for up to 15 days; the longer you keep it, the stronger the flavour.

MANGO PICKLE YOGURT

It's important to use mango pickle here, not mango chutney, which would be too sweet for this recipe. The oil-based pickle, or achar, is made with green mango, and tastes salty and sharp. We pair this yogurt with our Pea, Spinach & Potato Bondas (see page 54), but it's also great as a marinade for plant-based chick'n or served with roasted vegetables.

MAKES 500G (1LB 2OZ)

200G (7OZ) MANGO PURÉE

1 TABLESPOON AGAVE SYRUP

70G (2½OZ) HOT MANGO PICKLE

½ TABLESPOON FRESHLY CHOPPED CORIANDER

¼ RED BIRD'S EYE CHILLI, chopped

JUICE OF 1 LEMON

½ TEASPOON SALT

300G (10½OZ) COCONUT YOGURT

1) Place all the ingredients except the coconut yogurt in a blender or food processor and blend to combine.

2) Transfer the resulting paste to a bowl, then fold in the coconut yogurt. This is ready to use right away, and will keep in the fridge for up to 1 week.

QUICK PICKLED CUCUMBERS

Pickling is one of those surprisingly simple culinary skills that really impresses people. These sweet Middle Eastern-style pickles are a perfect complement to our Turkish-Style Brunch (see page 32) or grilled Arayes (see page 122).

1) Combine the vinegar, water and sugar in a saucepan over a medium–high heat. Bring to the boil and simmer for 5 minutes until all the sugar has dissolved, then take off the heat.

2) Cut the cucumbers into quarters lengthways, then place them vertically in a sterilised jar (see page 166). If they are too long to fit in the jar, cut them in half. Add the crushed seeds and chilli, sliced garlic and salt.

3) Pour the liquid into the jar, making sure the cucumbers are fully submerged, then seal. Leave the jar at room temperature for at least 12 hours (do not open the lid during this time). Once open, they will last for up to 1 week in the fridge.

MAKES 1 LITRE (1¾ PINTS)

200ML (7FL OZ) CIDER VINEGAR

200ML (7FL OZ) WATER

60G (2¼OZ) CASTER SUGAR

4 SMALL CUCUMBERS

1 TEASPOON CORIANDER SEEDS, crushed

1 TEASPOON FENNEL SEEDS, crushed

½ SMALL RED CHILLI, diced

1 GARLIC CLOVE, sliced

½ TEASPOON SALT

CHEF'S TIP

If you want a more intense flavour, leave the jar at room temperature for a week before sampling.

CARROT & LIME LEAF PICKLES

A simple and useful pickle preparation, these quick pickles are great for adding punch to salads or slaws, or as a fresh topping for lettuce cups or stir-fries. We use a mandoline for the julienned carrots, but you can also use a julienne peeler, which are very affordable. Failing that, the large side of a box grater works well too.

1) Combine the water, vinegar, sugar, ginger, turmeric, salt and lime leaves in a small saucepan over a low heat. Heat gently for 3 minutes, until the sugar crystals have just dissolved.

2) Take off the heat and add the carrots and chillies. Stir gently.

3) Allow to cool completely, then use straight away or store in a sterilised jar (see page 166) in the refrigerator for up to 5 days.

MAKES 600G (1LB 5OZ)

200ML (7FL OZ) WATER

100ML (3½FL OZ) RICE VINEGAR

40G (1½OZ) CASTER SUGAR

1 TEASPOON FINELY CHOPPED GINGER

PINCH OF GROUND TURMERIC

1 TEASPOON SALT

4 LIME LEAVES, deveined and very finely sliced

300G (10½OZ) CARROTS, peeled and julienned

2 SMALL RED BIRD'S EYE CHILLIES, finely sliced

Swap it! ⟶

If you can't get hold of lime leaves you can make this without, or use finely chopped lemon grass instead.

HERB BUTTER

If you're the type of person who likes to get ahead, this butter can be prepared in advance and kept in the freezer. Then you can just add it to pasta or use it to top a side of greens at a moment's notice, delivering an extra punch of flavour.

MAKES 250G (9OZ)
(8–10 PORTIONS)

250G (9OZ) PLANT-BASED
BUTTER, at room temperature,
chopped into cubes

20G (¾OZ) FLAT-LEAF
PARSLEY, leaves picked and
chopped

2 GARLIC CLOVES, finely
chopped or grated

ZEST AND JUICE OF
½ LEMON

½ TEASPOON SALT

1) Combine all the ingredients, either in a stand mixer fitted with the paddle attachment, or by hand using a spoon.

2) Once fully combined, scoop the flavoured butter out on to a sheet of baking parchment and roll it to form a log. Leave in the freezer to go solid. Once solid, it can be chopped into portioned slices and stored in a freezer bag or other freezer-proof container for up to 3 months.

CHEF'S TIP

This butter makes an excellent addition to pasta with a little fresh basil and halved cherry tomatoes.

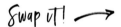

You can try this butter with so many kinds of herbs; just swap out the parsley for oregano or basil as desired. One of my favourites is sage butter, which I use with fresh tortelloni.

sweet

MOCHA POTS

These chocolate pots make a nice end to a grown-up meal (they contain a bit too much caffeine for kids) and are super simple to make. They look cute prepared in pretty cups and saucers if you have them, or you can use a classic dessert ramekin. They can be prepared as little as 1 hour before serving, or as much as 24 hours ahead, just to make life a bit easier.

SERVES 4–6

250ML (9FL OZ) PLANT-BASED CREAM

30G (1OZ) MUSCOVADO SUGAR

3CM (1¼IN) SLIVER OF VANILLA POD, seeds scraped

250G (9OZ) DARK CHOCOLATE, chopped into small pieces

1 SHOT (20ML/¾FL OZ) ESPRESSO

PINCH OF SALT

To serve

4 TABLESPOONS PLANT-BASED WHIPPING CREAM

GRATED DARK CHOCOLATE

1) Warm the cream, sugar and vanilla in a small saucepan over a medium heat for 5 minutes, stirring often, until the sugar has dissolved. Remove from the heat.

2) Pick out and discard the vanilla pod, then add the chopped chocolate, espresso and salt to the pan. Whisk to combine. If you have stick blender, blend the mixture for a couple of minutes so it becomes glossy. Otherwise, continue to whisk well by hand.

3) Divide the mixture between 4 cups or ramekins, or 6 espresso cups, and leave to set in the fridge for at least 1 hour.

4) When ready to serve, whip the cream and top each cup with the cream, then grate over some chocolate to finish.

CARROT CUP CAKES

There's something quite magical about making a cake in the microwave. This is a great activity to do with kids, as it's mostly spoon measuring and there are no hot ovens to deal with.

1) In a small bowl, combine the oil, brown sugar, vanilla, milk, flour, baking powder, cinnamon and salt. Stir or whisk to combine the ingredients until smooth. Fold in the grated carrot.

2) Transfer the mixture to 2 teacups or 1 large mug and microwave on high for 1 minute 30 seconds–2 minutes, or until the cake has stopped rising and is firm to the touch. If you're making the cake in teacups, you can cook them both at the same time if you have space in the microwave.

3) Allow to cool before topping with plant-based whipped cream, a dusting of cinnamon and some orange zest.

MAKES 2 TEACUP CAKES OR 1 BIG MUG CAKE

2 TABLESPOONS VEGETABLE OIL

3 TABLESPOONS SOFT LIGHT BROWN SUGAR

¼ TEASPOON VANILLA EXTRACT

3 TABLESPOONS SOY OR ALMOND MILK

5 TABLESPOONS SELF-RAISING FLOUR

½ TEASPOON BAKING POWDER

½ TEASPOON GROUND CINNAMON, plus extra to decorate

PINCH OF SALT

35G (1¼OZ) GRATED CARROT (1 small carrot)

For the topping

PLANT-BASED WHIPPED CREAM

ORANGE ZEST

PEACH MELBA PARFAIT

Perfect for a summer garden party, this freezer cake is very easy to prepare, but looks impressive. You can find fruit coulis in most supermarkets – look for the aisle where the ice cream accompaniments are sold. The parfait will hold for a surprisingly long time once it's out of the freezer, but it probably won't last for more than an hour, so don't take it out too long before eating.

SERVES 6–8

RAPESEED OIL, FOR GREASING

50G (1¾OZ) GINGER BISCUITS

250ML (9FL OZ) PLANT-BASED WHIPPING CREAM

2 TABLESPOONS GOLDEN SYRUP

1 TEASPOON VANILLA EXTRACT

2 RIPE PEACHES, pitted and finely sliced

150G (5½OZ) FRESH RASPBERRIES, halved, plus extra to decorate

100G (3½OZ) RASPBERRY COULIS, plus extra to decorate

MINT LEAVES, to decorate

Swap it! →

You can swap the peaches for nectarines or plums.

1) Lightly grease a 23cm (9in) loaf tin and generously line with clingfilm, making sure you have enough overhang to cover the top once the tin is full.

2) Break the ginger biscuits into pieces. You can do this by putting them into a freezer bag and smashing with something heavy, like a rolling pin.

3) In a large bowl, use an electric whisk to whip the plant-based cream with the golden syrup and vanilla extract until it forms soft peaks. Fold in the ginger biscuit pieces.

4) Arrange some of the peach slices and raspberries in the base of the loaf tin.

5) Fold the rest of the fruit into the cream mixture, then add the coulis, but just fold once or twice. Carefully transfer the mixture into the loaf tin, and bang the tin firmly on the counter so that it settles well. Wrap the cling film over the top and place in the freezer for at least 5 hours.

6) When it's time to serve, remove the tin from the freezer and leave it out on the side for 30 minutes before opening the cling film, then turning the parfait out on to a long, narrow plate or board.

7) Decorate the parfait with some more raspberries, an extra drizzle of coulis and a few mint leaves.

CRÈME BRÛLÉE

Vegan crème brûlée was a recipe we worked on for quite some time, and it was only possible with the massive improvement that has come about in plant-based creams. To finish this crème brûlée properly, you will need a little culinary blowtorch – they can be bought fairly inexpensively online. We set the crème brûlée with a vegan gelling agent, and the richness is provided by cocoa butter, so the overall feel is very luxurious. This is lovely served simply with some fresh berries.

1) Measure the cream into a jug and sprinkle over the gelling agent. Stir in the vanilla seeds and pod (or extract). Leave for 10 minutes to allow the gelling agent to activate.

2) Meanwhile, get 4–5 ramekins ready, arranging them on a level plate or small dish so they can be easily moved to the fridge. Prepare a jug with a small sieve, ready to strain the crème brûlée mixture once you have cooked it.

3) When everything is ready to go, pour the cream mixture into a saucepan over a low heat, along with the sugar and salt. Bring to the boil and boil for 10 minutes, then add the cocoa butter and stir through to melt.

4) Quickly strain the mixture into the jug, then pour it into the prepared ramekins and place in the fridge for at least 2 hours to cool completely.

5) When you're ready to serve, it's time to brûlée! Evenly scatter about ½ tablespoon sugar over the surface of the first ramekin. Use the blowtorch to melt the sugar until it is golden but not burning. Make sure you don't leave any un-torched sugar around the edges. Repeat with the other ramekins and wait 2 minutes before serving.

MAKES 4–5

500ML (18FL OZ) PLANT-BASED CREAM

3.25G (¹⁄₁₀OZ) VEGAN GELLING AGENT (we use ½ packet of Vegi Gel)

¼ VANILLA POD, deseeded, but keep the pod too (alternatively, use ½ teaspoon good-quality vanilla extract with seeds)

70G (2½OZ) CASTER SUGAR, plus extra to finish

PINCH OF SALT

1 TABLESPOON COCOA BUTTER

CARAMEL COOKIE CHEESECAKE WITH BROWN SUGAR BLACKBERRIES

This is a super-simplified version of one of our all-time best-selling desserts. With no oven involved, and very few ingredients, this is a little wonder recipe that takes only a few minutes of preparation. The blackberries provide a fresh and slightly acidic foil to the very rich cheesecake.

SERVES 6–8

200G (7OZ) LOTUS BISCOFF BISCUITS, broken into crumbs

80G (2¾OZ) PLANT-BASED BUTTER, melted

300G (10½OZ) FULL-FAT PLANT-BASED CREAM CHEESE

400G (14OZ) JAR OF LOTUS BISCOFF SPREAD

220ML (8FL OZ) PLANT-BASED CREAM

For the macerated berries

400G (14OZ) BLACKBERRIES, halved

150G (5½OZ) SOFT LIGHT BROWN SUGAR

JUICE OF 1 LEMON

1) Line the base and sides of a 20cm (8in) round springform cake tin with baking parchment.

2) In a bowl, combine the biscuit crumbs with the melted plant-based butter. Tip the mixture into the cake tin and press into the base in an even layer. Pop in the fridge for 30 minutes to chill.

3) Meanwhile, make the cheesecake filling. You can either do this in a stand mixer with the paddle attachment, or by hand in a bowl. Beat the plant-based cream cheese until fluffy, then add the Lotus Biscoff spread and plant-based cream and beat to form a smooth batter (don't mix too hard or for too long, or it will collapse).

4) Pour the cheesecake batter into the prepared cake tin, taking care not to disturb the biscuit base. Leave to set in the refrigerator for at least 2 hours.

5) Meanwhile, prepare the macerated blackberries. In a bowl, mix together the blackberries with the sugar and the lemon juice. Cover and leave to macerate so that the berries have time to naturally release their juices.

6) Slice the cheesecake and serve topped with the macerated blackberries.

DOUBLE-CHOCOLATE ICE-CREAM SANDWICHES

If you don't feel like making the cookies yourself, you can use shop-bought ones. The really fun bit is dipping the ice-cream sandwiches in the chocolate – that's definitely a part that kids will enjoy helping with (as well as licking the bowl, of course).

1) Arrange the cookies on a plate or tray. Scoop the softened ice cream on to 6 of the cookies, then top with the other 6 cookies. Wrap the cookie sandwiches in freezer bags and freeze for at least 3–4 hours.

2) Melt the chocolate in a heatproof bowl in the microwave in 20-second bursts, or in a heatproof bowl set over a pan of barely simmering water.

3) Line a tray with baking parchment. Dip the cookie sandwiches into the melted chocolate one at a time, then place on the prepared tray. Once they've all been dipped, return to the freezer for 30 minutes until the chocolate is firm, then serve.

SERVES 6

12 DARK CHOCOLATE CHIP & SEA SALT COOKIES (see page 214), or shop-bought vegan cookies

6 SCOOPS (ABOUT 375G/13OZ) PLANT-BASED VANILLA ICE CREAM, softened

300G (10½OZ) DARK CHOCOLATE CHIPS

BUTTERSCOTCH BANANA SPLIT

There is nothing more retro – or more fun – than a banana split. We have included some fancy extras here, like butterscotch sauce and a simple brandy snap recipe to create some stylish garnishes. If preparing this for children, skip the Scotch and the recipe will make a nice caramel sauce. Use whatever vegan ice cream flavour you prefer (except perhaps mint!).

SERVES 4

4 BANANAS

465ML (16FL OZ) TUB PLANT-BASED ICE CREAM

For the brandy snaps

50G (1¾OZ) PLANT-BASED BUTTER

50G (1¾OZ) SOFT LIGHT BROWN SUGAR

50G (1¾OZ) GOLDEN SYRUP

50G (1¾OZ) PLAIN FLOUR

⅛ TEASPOON GROUND GINGER

DASH OF BRANDY

For the butterscotch

110G (3¾OZ) PLANT-BASED BUTTER

150G (5½OZ) SOFT DARK BROWN SUGAR

¼ TEASPOON SEA SALT FLAKES

25ML (¾FL OZ) SCOTCH WHISKY

300ML (½ PINT) PLANT-BASED CREAM

To serve

PLANT-BASED WHIPPED CREAM

ROASTED HAZELNUTS, chopped

4 VEGAN GLACÉ CHERRIES

1) For the brandy snaps, melt the butter, sugar and golden syrup in a small saucepan over a low heat. Once melted and combined, take off the heat.

2) Mix together the flour and ground ginger in a mixing bowl, then make a well in the centre. Pour in the brandy, followed by the butter mixture, and gradually beat into the flour with a fork, until the mixture is fully combined and forms a dough. Place the dough in the fridge for 30 minutes.

3) Preheat the oven to 180°C/160°C fan/350°F/ gas mark 4 and line a baking tray with baking parchment.

4) Once the dough has chilled, scoop out 8 balls of about 15g (½oz) each. (Keep the rest of the dough to use another time. It will keep for up to 1 week in the fridge or up to 3 months in the freezer.) Place the balls of biscuit dough on the prepared baking tray, spacing them apart, as they will spread. Bake them for 8–10 minutes until golden brown and set, then leave to cool completely for 10–15 minutes.

5) Meanwhile, to make the butterscotch, melt the butter in a small saucepan over low heat. Add the sugar and stir with a wooden spoon to combine, then add the salt. Add the Scotch and let the liquid evaporate, then pour in the cream. Cook for 5–7 minutes, whisking very occasionally – no more than every few minutes. The sauce should become slightly darker in colour, but won't seem very thick (it will thicken as it cools). Transfer into a container and let it cool slightly.

6) To assemble the banana splits, peel the bananas and slice them in half lengthways. Place 2 banana halves along either side of a long, narrow, shallow dish. Arrange 3 scoops of plant-based ice cream between the banana slices, then top with plant-based whipped cream. Drizzle over the butterscotch, then finish with the chopped hazelnuts, 2 brandy snaps and a glacé cherry. Repeat for the other splits.

CHOCOLATE BARK

If you're not really into baking or making cakes, chocolate bark is the ideal way to prepare a sweet end to a meal with minimal effort. We've suggested two topping ideas, but really you can use any dried fruits and roasted nuts you want. To serve, just smash the bark into chunks and let people nibble away while having tea or coffee.

PEANUT BUTTER CHOCOLATE BARK

200G (7OZ) VEGAN CHOCOLATE

2 TABLESPOONS PEANUT BUTTER, thinned with a little water

35G (1¼OZ) SALTED PEANUTS, chopped

ABOUT 20 HARD MINI PRETZELS

1 TEASPOON FREEZE-DRIED RASPBERRIES

1) Line a baking tray with baking parchment.

2) Melt the chocolate in a heatproof bowl in the microwave in 20-second bursts, or in a heatproof bowl set over a pan of barely simmering water.

3) Scoop the melted chocolate on to the prepared tray and spread out into a thin layer about 4mm (¼in) thick.

4) Drizzle the peanut butter over the chocolate and swirl it in a bit, then scatter over the peanuts, pretzels and freeze-dried raspberries.

5) Leave the bark to cool before smashing and serving.

TROPICAL BARK

200G (7OZ) VEGAN CHOCOLATE

1 TABLESPOON BANANA CHIPS

1 TABLESPOON DRIED MANGO

1 TABLESPOON DRIED PINEAPPLE

½ TABLESPOON GOJI BERRIES

½ TABLESPOON CRYSTALLISED GINGER, sliced

A SPRINKLING OF EDIBLE FLOWERS

1) Line a baking tray with baking parchment.

2) Melt the chocolate in a heatproof bowl in the microwave in 20-second bursts, or in a heatproof bowl set over a pan of barely simmering water.

3) Scoop the melted chocolate on to the prepared tray and spread out into a thin layer about 4mm (¼in) thick.

4) Scatter the banana chips, dried mango, dried pineapple, goji berries and crystallised ginger over the top, then press the edible flowers into any gaps.

5) Leave the bark to cool before smashing and serving.

SEE IMAGE, OVERLEAF ➜

peanut butter
chocolate bark

Tropical bark →

LEMON PANNA COTTA WITH BLACK CHERRY COMPOTE

The gentle lemon zing of this classic Italian dessert makes this a refreshingly light finish to a meal. You can buy great-quality ready-made cherry compote, which makes this recipe even easier, but if you do make your own, we think you'll enjoy the acidity of the pomegranate molasses we've used here. If you prepare and serve these panna cottas in glasses, then you don't have to worry about turning them out.

SERVES 3–4

500ML (18FL OZ) PLANT-BASED CREAM

3.25G ($\frac{1}{10}$OZ) VEGAN GELLING AGENT (we use ½ packet of Vegi Gel)

ZEST OF 1 LEMON

50G (1¾OZ) CASTER SUGAR, plus extra to finish

PINCH OF SALT

ORANGE ZEST, to decorate

For the black cherry compote

200G (7OZ) BLACK CHERRIES, pitted (frozen and defrosted cherries are fine, but we don't recommend canned)

JUICE OF 1 LEMON

50G (1¾OZ) CASTER SUGAR

2 TABLESPOONS POMEGRANATE MOLASSES

1 TEASPOON CORNFLOUR

1) Pour the cream into a jug and sprinkle over the gelling agent. Leave for 10 minutes to allow the gelling agent to activate. Meanwhile, get 3–4 ramekins ready, arranging them on a level plate or small dish so they can be easily moved to the fridge. Prepare a jug with a small sieve, ready to strain the panna cotta mixture once you have cooked it.

2) When everything is ready to go, pour the cream mixture into a saucepan over a low heat, along with the lemon zest, sugar and salt. Bring to the boil and boil for 10 minutes, then strain the mixture into the jug to remove the lemon zest and then pour the mixture into the prepared ramekins. Transfer to the refrigerator and leave to set for at least 2 hours.

3) To make the black cherry compote, combine the cherries, lemon juice, sugar and pomegranate molasses in a saucepan over a low heat and bring to a simmer. If using fresh cherries, you may need to add a splash of water. Simmer for 3–4 minutes until all the sugar is dissolved and the mixture has slightly reduced.

4) In a small bowl or mug, combine the cornflour with a splash of water to make a paste. Add the cornflour paste to the cherry mixture and cook for 5 minutes until thickened, then take off the heat. As the black cherry compote cools, the cherries will release some more juice, making the compote a bit thinner.

5) Once the compote is completely cool (this will take about 20 minutes), drizzle it over the panna cotta and serve, decorated with orange zest.

CHOCOLATE & ALMOND MEDJOOL DATES

A real splash of luxury, these stuffed dates are nice enough to serve as dessert or to present as a gift. If you don't have Medjool dates, you can use any whole dried stone fruit, such as prunes or apricots. You can decorate these with all kinds of pretty things, like chopped pistachios or other nuts, rose petals, sea salt crystals or cocoa nibs. We like to use freeze-dried raspberries, which add a nice touch of colour.

1) Line a baking tray with baking parchment.

2) To make the almond paste, combine all the ingredients in a bowl and mix well with a spoon, or blend in a blender.

3) Make a small incision in each of the dates and remove the stones and hard stems.

4) Divide the almond paste into 10–12 balls, then roll these into little sausage shapes the size of the dates. Open the dates and fill with the almond paste portions, then smooth over with your finger.

5) Melt the chocolate in a heatproof bowl in the microwave in 20-second bursts, or in a heatproof bowl set over a pan of barely simmering water.

6) Using something sharp, like a kebab skewer, skewer one of the dates and dip it into the chocolate, using a spoon to help coat the date. Let all the excess chocolate drip off then place on the prepared tray. Repeat with the remaining dates, then scatter over your chosen decorations while the chocolate is still warm.

MAKES 10–12

10–12 MEDJOOL DATES

150G (5½OZ) DARK CHOCOLATE, chopped into small pieces, OR DARK CHOCOLATE CHIPS

For the almond paste

2 TABLESPOONS AGAVE SYRUP

1 TABLESPOON ALMOND BUTTER

60G (2OZ) GROUND ALMONDS

½ TEASPOON VANILLA EXTRACT

PINCH OF SALT

To decorate

ANYTHING YOU LIKE – WE LIKE FREEZE-DRIED RASPBERRIES, PISTACHIOS, SEA SALT FLAKES OR EDIBLE GOLD POWDER

bakes

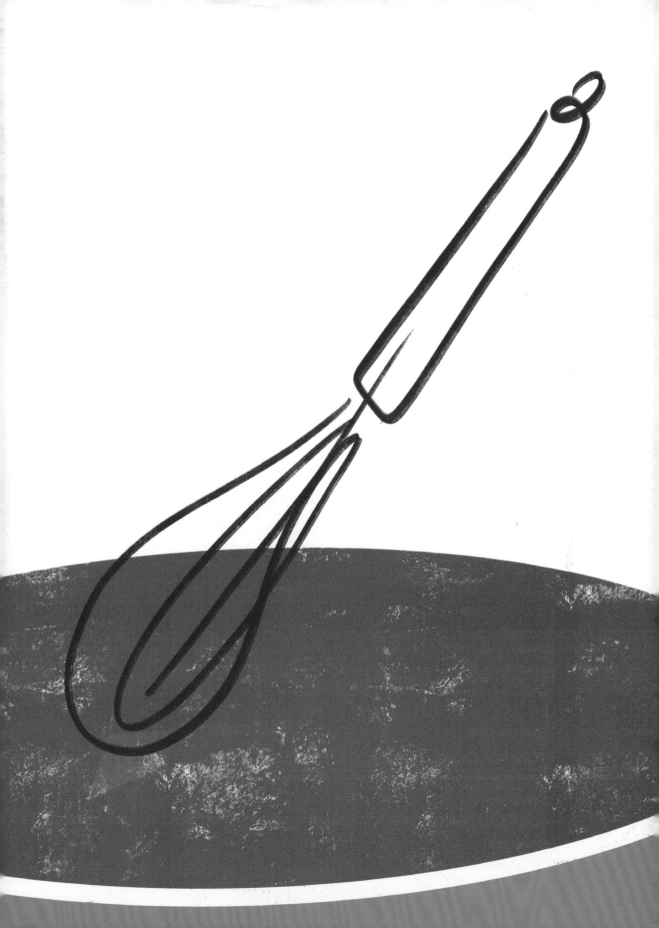

LEMON & LAVENDER DRIZZLE CAKE

The ultimate loaf cake, a lemon drizzle is a perennially popular addition to any teatime. We are torn between lemon icing and a crunchy lemon-sugar finish. If you prefer icing, go for icing sugar; if you're a fan of the crunch, opt for granulated sugar (see Chef's tip, below).

SERVES 6–8

For the dry ingredients

275G (9¼OZ) SELF-RAISING FLOUR

60G (2¼OZ) GROUND ALMONDS

180G (6½OZ) CASTER SUGAR

½ TABLESPOON BAKING POWDER

PINCH OF SALT

1 TEASPOON CRUSHED LAVENDER, plus extra to decorate

For the wet ingredients

100ML (3½FL OZ) RAPESEED OIL, plus extra for greasing

225ML (8FL OZ) SOY OR ALMOND MILK

1 TABLESPOON COCONUT YOGURT

ZEST OF 3–4 LEMONS, PLUS 2 TABLESPOONS JUICE

1 TEASPOON VANILLA EXTRACT

TINY PINCH OF GROUND TURMERIC (optional)

For the lemon icing

175G (6OZ) ICING SUGAR

PINCH OF SALT

5 TEASPOONS LEMON JUICE

To decorate

HALVED BLUEBERRIES

LEMON ZEST

EDIBLE FLOWERS

1) Preheat the oven to 180°C/160°C fan/350°F/gas mark 4. Grease a 900g (2lb) loaf tin and line with baking parchment.

2) Weigh out the dry ingredients into a large bowl and mix well to combine.

3) Measure the wet ingredients and pour into a jug.

4) Pour the wet ingredients into the dry, then mix well to combine. Pour the batter into the prepared tin and drag a knife down the length of the cake, about 3cm (1¼in) deep. This will help the cake form a split line down the centre.

5) Bake the cake for 30–35 minutes until golden and well risen, and a skewer inserted into the middle comes out clean. Leave to cool in the tin for 15 minutes, then transfer to a wire rack to cool completely.

6) To make the lemon icing, combine the icing sugar and salt with the lemon juice and mix really well, then drizzle over the cake. Scatter over the lavender, halved blueberries, lemon zest and edible flowers before serving.

7) The cake will keep in the fridge for up to 5 days.

CHEF'S TIP

If you prefer a simple sugar drizzle, then combine 100g (3½oz) granulated sugar with 1 tablespoon lemon juice and stir until the sugar crystals have dissolved. Pour over the cake while still warm.

Swap it! ⟶

If you like rose, leave out the lavender and instead add rose water to the mixture and the icing, to taste, then decorate with rose petals.

GINGER STICKY TOFFEE PUDDING WITH TOFFEE SAUCE

The ultimate comfort dessert, sticky toffee pudding is perfect for a rainy Sunday lunch, yet special enough to serve at an occasion. We've tried plenty of different recipes for sticky toffee pudding, experimenting with apple sauce or mashed bananas, before realising that dates are all we need to keep this dessert distinctively moist and soft. The ginger isn't overpowering; it just adds a subtle undertone of gentle spice that works really well in this delicious pudding.

1) Preheat the oven to 180°C/160°C fan/350°F/ gas mark 4. Grease a 20cm (8in) square baking tin and line with baking parchment.

2) Heat the milk, dates and ginger in a small saucepan over a low heat for a few minutes, whisking as they heat. The mixture should be thick and caramel coloured. Leave to rest in the pan.

3) In a stand mixer fitted with the paddle attachment, or in a bowl using an electric whisk, whisk the butter and sugar until pale and fluffy. Add the flour and mix well to form a smooth batter.

4) Add the date molasses, ground ginger, bicarbonate of soda and baking powder to the saucepan containing the date mixture, and whisk to combine. Fold this date mixture into the bowl of batter, then pour into the prepared tin. Smooth the top and bake for 35 minutes until the centre of the pudding is well risen and a skewer inserted into the middle comes out clean.

5) Meanwhile, make the toffee sauce. In a small saucepan over a low heat, combine the butter, sugar and date molasses for 3–5 minutes until you have a dark-coloured toffee sauce. Add the ginger and whisk through.

6) In a small bowl or mug, mix the cornflour with a splash of water to create a paste. Add this to the sauce, along with the cream and salt, and cook gently for 2 minutes more until thickened.

7) Once the pudding has finished baking, leave it to rest for 5 minutes, then spoon over enough of the toffee sauce to give it a thin, shiny coating.

8) Serve the pudding warm, with the rest of the toffee sauce in a jug on the side, along with plant-based cream, ice cream, custard or all three!

SERVES 9

140G (5OZ) PLANT-BASED BUTTER, plus extra for greasing

375ML (12½FL OZ) SOY MILK

220G (8OZ) DATES, chopped

1 TEASPOON GRATED GINGER

140G (5OZ) SOFT DARK BROWN SUGAR

225G (8OZ) SELF-RAISING FLOUR

2½ TABLESPOONS DATE MOLASSES

2 TEASPOONS GROUND GINGER

½ TABLESPOON BICARBONATE OF SODA

1 TEASPOON BAKING POWDER

PLANT-BASED CREAM, ICE CREAM OR CUSTARD, to serve

For the toffee sauce

40G (1½OZ) PLANT-BASED BUTTER

100G (3½OZ) SOFT DARK BROWN SUGAR

2 TABLESPOONS DATE MOLASSES

¼ TEASPOON GROUND GINGER

½ TABLESPOON CORNFLOUR

150ML (¼ PINT) PLANT-BASED CREAM

PINCH OF SALT

DARK CHOCOLATE CHIP & SEA SALT COOKIES

The best chocolate chip cookies are golden and crisp on the edges and chewy in the middle. There is a very simple trick to ensuring that you get this result, which is easy but requires patience. If you cook the dough straight away, the cookies will puff in the middle and then collapse and either taste dry or cakey. However, if you allow the dough to rest in the fridge for 24–48 hours, the gluten has time to form, meaning the middle will be both fully cooked and gooey. The rolls of cookie dough can be cut into slices and stored in the freezer, which means you can have freshly baked cookies whenever you want them.

MAKES 2 ROLLS OF COOKIE DOUGH OR 16 COOKIES

275G (9¾OZ) PLANT-BASED BUTTER, at room temperature

100G (3½OZ) CASTER SUGAR

300G (10½OZ) SOFT LIGHT BROWN SUGAR

1 TABLESPOON VANILLA EXTRACT

90ML (6 TABLESPOONS) SOY MILK

300G (10½OZ) PLAIN FLOUR

240G (8½OZ) STRONG WHITE BREAD FLOUR

¼ TEASPOON BICARBONATE OF SODA

1 TEASPOON SEA SALT FLAKES, plus extra to decorate

300G (10½OZ) DARK CHOCOLATE CHIPS

1) In a large bowl, beat together the butter, both sugars and the vanilla extract until pale and fluffy. Alternatively, use a stand mixer, making sure you scrape down the sides of the bowl.

2) Slowly add the milk, beating between each addition until well incorporated.

3) In a separate bowl, combine both flours with the bicarbonate of soda, salt and chocolate chips. Add the flour mixture to the butter mixture and beat slowly to combine until you have a thick dough with no lumps of flour left.

4) Cut out 2 long sheets of baking parchment. Separate the dough into 2 balls, then shape each one into a roll and roll tightly in the baking parchment. The rolls should be about 10cm (4in) in diameter. Twist the ends of the baking parchment so the rolls are tightly closed, then chill in the fridge for 24–48 hours.

5) When you're ready to bake, preheat the oven to 180°C/160°C fan/350°F/gas mark 4 and line 2 baking trays with baking parchment.

6) Cut the cookie dough into discs of around 50g (1¾oz) each (about 1cm/½in thick) and arrange on the prepared trays, spacing them out evenly and pressing them down slightly.

7) Bake for 10–15 minutes until golden around the edges but not browning, then cool for 10 minutes before eating. If baking from frozen, allow to defrost on the tray for 10 minutes, then bake for 18 minutes. Decorate with a sprinkling of sea salt flakes. These are best consumed warm with a cold glass of plant-based milk.

GINGER MOLASSES COOKIES

These comforting classic cookies are also known as Molly's. I first came across Molly's in North Carolina 20 years ago, but they go back to the 1800s and are an American classic. I think I prefer them to chocolate chip cookies, because they are easier to make and have a lovely crunchy-on-the-outside-and-gooey-on-the-inside finish, which is, of course, the gold standard by which cookies are measured. Super simple to make and really cosy to eat, especially with a warm cup of tea or chai.

MAKES 16

115G (4OZ) PLANT-BASED BUTTER, at room temperature

200G (7OZ) CASTER SUGAR

60G (2¼OZ) MOLASSES OR TREACLE

20G (¾OZ) AQUAFABA (see page 233)

225G (8OZ) PLAIN FLOUR

1 TEASPOON BICARBONATE OF SODA

1 TEASPOON GROUND GINGER

½ TEASPOONS GROUND CINNAMON

¼ TEASPOON SALT

1) Preheat the oven to 180°C/160°C fan/350°F/gas mark 4 and line 2 baking trays with baking parchment.

2) In a stand mixer fitted with the paddle attachment, or in a bowl with a wooden spoon, beat together the butter and 150g (5½oz) of the sugar until creamy. Add the molasses or treacle and aquafaba and mix well.

3) Sift in the flour, bicarbonate of soda, spices and salt and mix well to combine.

4) Scatter the remaining 50g (1¾oz) sugar into a bowl. Using a teaspoon, scoop up walnut-sized lumps of the cookie dough and roll them between your hands, then drop into the sugar to coat. Place on the prepared baking trays, spacing them at least 7cm (2¾in) apart so they have plenty of room to spread.

5) Bake for 10 minutes until golden brown, then leave to cool on a wire rack. These will keep well in an airtight container for up to 5 days.

FRESH STRAWBERRIES & CREAM VICTORIA SPONGE

It's said that Queen Victoria was a big fan of afternoon teas, expecting a variety of sponge cakes to be served. Baking powder was invented during her reign, making it even easier to make the light sponge that bears her name. Conventionally, the cream is served in the centre of the cake, but whipped plant-based cream is a lot less firm than its dairy counterpart, and so it is a safer bet to pile the cream on top.

1) Preheat oven to 180°C/160°C fan/350°F/gas mark 4 and line 2 × 20cm (8in) round cake tins.

2) In a large bowl, combine the wet ingredients and leave to rest for 5 minutes while you prepare the dry ingredients.

3) In a separate large bowl, mix together the dry ingredients.

4) Add the wet mixture to the dry mixture and whisk to create a smooth batter. Pour this into the prepared cake tins and bake for 35 minutes until the cakes are well risen and a skewer inserted into the centres comes out clean.

5) Cool the cakes in the tins for 10 minutes, then transfer to a wire rack to cool completely.

6) Once cool, choose the prettiest sponge to be the top. Spread the jam over the other one, then arrange some of the sliced strawberries over the jam. Place the other sponge on top and dust liberally with icing sugar.

7) When ready to serve, whip the plant-based cream until fluffy, then whip in the icing sugar. Pile the cream on top of the cake and decorate with the remaining strawberries, mint and a dusting of icing sugar.

CHEF'S TIP

If you only have one cake tin, you can bake all of the batter in one tin for 50–55 minutes, then slice it in half once cool.

SEE IMAGE, OVERLEAF ➞

SERVES 2

For the wet ingredients

250ML (9FL OZ) SOY MILK

1 TEASPOON GOOD-QUALITY VANILLA EXTRACT

1 TABLESPOON LEMON JUICE

1½ TABLESPOONS COCONUT YOGURT

120ML (4FL OZ) LIGHT OIL, such as sunflower or rapeseed oil

For the dry ingredients

325G (11½OZ) SELF-RAISING FLOUR

250G (9OZ) CASTER SUGAR

PINCH OF SALT

TINY PINCH OF TURMERIC (optional)

1 TABLESPOON BAKING POWDER

To decorate

200G (7OZ) STRAWBERRY JAM

250G (9OZ) STRAWBERRIES, sliced

2 TABLESPOONS ICING SUGAR, sifted, plus extra for the top

125ML (4FL OZ) PLANT-BASED WHIPPING CREAM

MINT SPRIGS

Swap it! →

If you want a buttercream filling instead of fresh cream, then making vegan buttercream is similar to making the conventional stuff. Just cream together 100g (3½oz) softened plant-based butter with 200g (7oz) sifted icing sugar until fluffy, adding a couple of spoonfuls of plant-based milk if necessary. This can be spread on the inside of the cooled cake.

CHAI MASALA BANANA BREAD

A perfect addition to any teatime or brunch table, banana bread is the ideal cake to make in advance. The masala chai-inspired spices in this bake will be especially good if left to develop for a day. When serving for breakfast, try toasting a couple of slices in a dry frying pan and then serving with coconut yogurt, some fruit slices and a drizzle of maple syrup.

1) Preheat oven to 180°C/160°C fan/350°F/gas mark 4. Grease a 900g (2lb) loaf tin with a little oil and line with baking parchment.

2) In a bowl, mash the bananas, then add the syrup and whisk together lightly, leaving the mixture a bit chunky. Stir in the oil.

3) In a separate bowl, combine the sugar, flour, spices, baking powder and salt and pepper and mix well. Tip the dry mixture into the wet mixture and mix together well with a whisk, working quite quickly.

4) Using a spatula, scrap the mixture into the prepared tin and smooth the surface slightly. If you like, you can drag a knife down the length of the cake, about 3cm (1¼in) deep. This will help the cake form a split line down the centre. Alternatively, you can arrange some long slices of banana over the top.

5) Bake for 55 minutes–1 hour in the middle of the oven until a skewer inserted into the centre comes out clean. Brush the top with a little maple syrup to glaze. Cool in the tin for 10 minutes, then transfer to a wire rack to cool completely. The cake will keep for 5 days in an airtight container at room temperature.

CHEF'S TIP

If you don't have super-ripe bananas, you can recreate the ripening process by baking the unpeeled bananas in the preheated oven for 10 minutes until the skins darken. Cool before peeling and mashing.

SERVES 6–8

160ML (5½FL OZ) VEGETABLE OIL, plus extra for greasing

320G (11OZ) VERY RIPE BANANAS, peeled, plus 1 extra, sliced lengthways, to decorate (optional)

2 TABLESPOONS MAPLE SYRUP, plus extra to glaze

120G (4¼OZ) CASTER SUGAR

250G (9OZ) SELF-RAISING FLOUR

½ TEASPOON GROUND CINNAMON

½ TEASPOON GROUND GINGER

SEEDS FROM 4 CARDAMOM PODS, crushed with a pestle and mortar, or ½ teaspoon ground cardamom

1 TEASPOON BAKING POWDER

PINCH OF SALT

PINCH OF FRESHLY GROUND BLACK PEPPER

To serve

COCONUT YOGURT

FRESH FRUIT, such as sliced mango and kiwi and halved grapes

FAUX-RERRO FUDGE CELEBRATION CAKE

Fudgy and squishy, this cake is a beast. A good chocolate cake is essential for celebrations and birthdays, and here the hazelnut-chocolate frosting adds a real touch of luxury.

SERVES 8–10

For the wet ingredients

450ML (16FL OZ) ALMOND MILK

1 TABLESPOON MAPLE SYRUP

1 TABLESPOON CIDER VINEGAR

180ML (6FL OZ) LIGHT VEGETABLE OIL

1 TEASPOON VANILLA EXTRACT

For the dry ingredients

110G (3¾OZ) COCOA POWDER

320G (11OZ) SELF-RAISING FLOUR

400G (14OZ) SOFT LIGHT BROWN SUGAR

PINCH OF SALT

For the frosting

130G (4¾OZ) PLANT-BASED BUTTER, at room temperature

300G (10½OZ) ICING SUGAR

40G (1½OZ) COCOA POWDER

200G (7OZ) VEGAN CHOCOLATE HAZELNUT SPREAD

40G (1½OZ) ROASTED CHOPPED HAZELNUTS, plus extra to decorate

PINCH OF SALT

3–5 TABLESPOONS PLANT-BASED CREAM

CHOCOLATE SHAVINGS, to decorate

1) Preheat the oven to 180°C/160°C fan/350°F/ gas mark 4 and line 2 × 20cm (8in) round cake tins with baking parchment.

2) Combine all the wet ingredients in a large jug and mix well with a whisk.

3) For the dry ingredients, sift the cocoa powder and flour into a large bowl, then stir in the sugar and salt.

4) Pour the wet mixture into the dry mixture and whisk to form a smooth batter with no lumps.

5) Divide the batter between the prepared tins and bake for 25–30 minutes until the cakes are well risen and a skewer inserted into the centre comes out clean. Leave to cool in the tins for 10 minutes, before transferring to a wire rack to cool completely.

6) To make the frosting, beat the butter using an electric whisk or in a stand mixer on medium speed for about 2 minutes until smooth. Sift in the icing sugar and cocoa powder and beat until creamy and smooth. Add the chocolate hazelnut spread, along with the nuts and salt, and mix to combine. Finally, slowly add the plant-based cream, a little at a time, until you have a creamy, spreadable texture. Increase the speed to medium–high and beat for another minute or so until fluffy. Vegan hazelnut spreads vary a bit, so if your mixture is too thin, you can add a little more icing sugar; if it's too thick, you can add a little more cream.

7) When the cakes are cool, spread half the frosting over the bottom cake, then put the other cake on top. Spread the rest of the frosting over the top of the cake, then decorate with the hazelnuts and chocolate shavings. This cake will keep for up to 5 days in an airtight container in the fridge.

Swap it! →

If you would like to make this cake for someone who has a nut-free diet, replace the almond milk with soy, and replace the frosting with chocolate buttercream using 200g (7oz) plant-based butter, 400g (14oz) icing sugar, 50g (1¾oz) cocoa powder and enough cold plant-based milk to achieve the desired consistency.

CHEF'S TIP

If you have just one cake tin, this will still work. Just bake all of the batter in one tin for 45–50 minutes until well risen, then slice in half once cool.

drinks

PINK ROSE LEMONADE

Elegant and refreshing, this is a perfect twist on the classic lemonade. I love rose, but it's not for everyone, so if you omit the rosewater, the raspberry will shine through, making this an excellent simple pink lemonade recipe. This pairs well with our Persian-Style Jackfruit & Walnut Wraps (see page 129) for a fragrant lunch in the garden.

SERVES 4

400ML (14FL OZ) WATER

2 TEASPOONS ROSEWATER

PINCH OF DRIED ROSE PETALS

100ML (3½FL OZ) AGAVE SYRUP

JUICE OF 4 LEMONS

75G (2¾OZ) RASPBERRIES, plus extra to serve

To serve

ICE

SODA WATER

THYME SPRIGS

FRESH EDIBLE ROSE PETALS (optional)

1) In a saucepan, combine the water, rosewater and rose petals over a low heat. Bring to a simmer for a couple of minutes, then take off the heat.

2) In a large jug, mix the agave with the lemon juice. Add the raspberries and smash them with a spoon to break them up.

3) Once the rosewater mixture has cooled, strain it into the jug and stir.

4) Refrigeraten the lemonade for at least 24 hours before serving – this will help to intensify the lemon and raspberry flavours.

5) When you're ready to serve, strain to remove the raspberry pips, then pour the lemonade into glasses with ice and top up with soda water. Garnish with thyme sprigs, rose petals (if using) and fresh raspberries.

LUXURY HOT CHOCOLATE

This is more of a dessert than a drink, and is the perfect solution if you want a simple way to get an indulgent chocolate hit at the end of a meal. In many countries, hot chocolate is drunk in the afternoon, as a delicious way to lift your spirits and ease you into the evening.

1) In a small bowl, combine the cocoa powder, sugar, vanilla extract and salt, and bring together with a whisk, adding just enough milk to make a smooth, thin paste.

2) Pour this mixture into a medium-sized saucepan and add most of the rest of the milk (just hold back a couple of tablespoons), along with the cream. Place over a low heat and warm through gently until it is just starting to simmer, whisking the mixture frequently.

3) Meanwhile, in a bowl, combine the cornflour with the remaining plant milk to form a paste and add this to the saucepan. Cook for another 2–3 minutes until slightly glossy and thickened.

4) Take off the heat and whisk in the chocolate pieces, then serve topped with whipped cream and marshmallows and decorated with extra cocoa powder.

CHEF'S TIP

It's fun to top this with torched vegan marshmallows. For this, you will need a little catering blowtorch; they are quite cheap to buy and really fun to use.

SERVES 4

4 TABLESPOONS COCOA POWDER, plus extra to decorate

2 TABLESPOONS SOFT LIGHT BROWN SUGAR

1 TEASPOON VANILLA EXTRACT

PINCH OF SALT

250ML (9FL OZ) BARISTA-STYLE PLANT-BASED MILK OF YOUR CHOICE

250ML (9FL OZ) PLANT-BASED CREAM

½ TEASPOON CORNFLOUR

75G (2¾OZ) DARK CHOCOLATE, broken into pieces

To decorate

PLANT-BASED WHIPPED CREAM

VEGAN MARSHMALLOWS

EASY WATERMELON SHRUB

The real taste of summer in a glass, this watermelon shrub recipe makes a refreshing cooler. The term 'shrub' means a mildly fermented drink made using vinegar, fruit, aromatics and sugar, and they are thought to aid digestion while having a pleasant tang. They're perfect for when you have guests and you need something super quick to prepare that's fun and impressive. You can prepare the shrub in advance and then top it up with ice and coconut water to make a pretty jug. This is a lovely paring for spicy snacks like our Pea, Spinach & Potato Bondas (see page 54) or Tempeh Larb (see pages 50–1).

MAKES 750ML (25FL OZ)

1KG (2LB 4OZ) RIPE WATERMELON FLESH (ABOUT 1 MEDIUM-SIZED WATERMELON), chopped into chunks

100ML (3½FL OZ) AGAVE SYRUP

100ML (3½FL OZ) GOOD-QUALITY APPLE CIDER VINEGAR

1) Put the watermelon chunks into the blender and blend to form a purée.

2) Strain the purée through a sieve into a jug. Add the agave and vinegar and stir until the agave has dissolved.

3) Pour into a glass or ceramic container, cover and store in the fridge for 1–2 days before using. This will keep for up to 5 days; the vinegary taste will disappear over time.

WATERMELON COOLER

SERVES 2

350ML (12FL OZ) EASY WATERMELON SHRUB (see above)

300ML (12FL OZ) COCONUT WATER OR SODA WATER

ICE CUBES

FRESH MINT LEAVES

1) Pour the shrub and coconut water or soda into a jug of ice cubes and serve garnished with mint leaves.

———

CHEF'S TIP

This also makes a great base for a cocktail. Pair with a fairly neutral white spirit, like vodka or white rum.

JASMINE & LEMONGRASS COLD-BREW ICED TEA

This is a refined, delicate take on iced tea that's full of fragrance. We use an excellent-quality jasmine tea at the restaurant, and we really recommend you source your tea carefully, as it makes all the difference to the end result. We haven't sweetened the tea here, but you may want to offer a neutral syrup, like light agave, if your guests have a sweet tooth.

SERVES 4–6

10G (¼OZ) LOOSE-LEAF JASMINE TEA

1 LEMON GRASS STALK, bashed with a rolling pin

1 LITRE (1¾ PINTS) WATER

ICE CUBES

LEMON RIND, cut into strips, or **CUCUMBER,** peeled into long ribbons, to decorate

1) Combine the tea, lemon grass and water in a large jar or jug. Cover and refrigerate overnight.

2) The next day, remove the lemon grass and strain the tea.

3) Serve the cold-brew tea over ice, with lemon rind strips or cucumber ribbons to decorate the glasses.

CHEF'S TIP

To serve this as a refreshing cocktail, add a shot of good-quality gin.

LYCHEE ROSE MARTINI

This fragrant, elegant martini has remained popular on our menu for years. It is the perfect accompaniment to a light meal. We use aquafaba to create the light, fluffy foam. If you aren't familiar with aquafaba, it's the protein-rich water strained off chickpeas and beans. These days you can buy it in a carton, or just strain it off a can of chickpeas. It is a perfect replacement for the egg white used in traditional cocktail recipes.

1) Pour the gin, lychee juice, lime juice and rosewater into a cocktail shaker and shake to combine, then add the aquafaba and shake hard for 1 minute.

2) Strain the cocktail into cold martini glasses and decorate with the rose petals and lychees.

CHEF'S TIP

If you do not have a cocktail shaker, you can use a jar.

MAKES 4

160ML (5½FL OZ) GIN

160ML (5½FL OZ) LYCHEE JUICE

1 TABLESPOON LIME JUICE

25ML (1FL OZ) ROSEWATER

1 TABLESPOON AQUAFABA

To decorate
EDIBLE ROSE PETALS
FRESH LYCHEES

SEE IMAGE, OVERLEAF →

PINEAPPLE NEGRONI

Legend has it that the negroni originated in Florence, the city of dreams – and this pineapple negroni is, indeed, the cocktail of your dreams. The pineapple gives the drink a sour yet sweet taste that provides a perfect balance to the bitters.

MAKES 2–4

100ML (3½FL OZ) GIN

100ML (3½FL OZ) VEGAN BITTER APERITIF (we like Carpano Bitters)

100ML (3½FL OZ) VEGAN SWEET VERMOUTH

100ML (3½FL OZ) PINEAPPLE JUICE

ICE CUBES

PINEAPPLE LEAF, to decorate

1) Combine the gin, bitter aperitif, sweet vermouth and pineapple juice in a cocktail shaker filled with ice, then shake.

2) Pour into 2–4 short glasses, decorate each with a pineapple leaf and serve.

––––––––––

CHEF'S TIP

For a 'party batch' of 1 litre (25fl oz), simply multiply all the ingredients by 10. Combine in a jug or bottle and refrigerate prior to serving. Serve over ice in measures of 100ml (3½fl oz).

COQUITO

In Spanish, *coquito* means 'little coconut', which is a super-cute name for this rich, creamy Puerto Rican cocktail. It is traditionally drunk at Christmas, a bit like a tropical eggnog. It makes a lovely way to finish a meal.

1) Place all the ingredients except the rum into a blender and blend to a purée. Pour into a large bottle and add the rum, then shake well to combine. Store in the fridge for 4 hours before serving; this will help to thicken the *coquito*, and will also help the flavours meld together.

2) To serve, dip the rims of 4 tumblers in agave syrup. Scatter the desiccated coconut on to a plate, then dip the rims of the tumblers in the coconut to decorate. Pour the cold *coquito* into the decorated glasses, and top with a pinch of ground cinnamon.

SERVES 4

400ML (14FL OZ) CAN COCONUT MILK

370ML (12½FL OZ) CAN VEGAN CONDENSED MILK

180ML (6FL OZ) PLANT-BASED CREAM

PINCH OF GROUND CINNAMON, plus extra to decorate

PINCH OF GROUND NUTMEG

½ TEASPOON VANILLA EXTRACT

250ML (9FL OZ) DARK RUM

To serve

AGAVE SYRUP

DESICCATED COCONUT

JALAPEÑO MARGARITA

We've had a lot of different margaritas on our cocktail menu over the years, and they are always bestsellers, so we're pretty confident this will be a hit at your next party. It's simple to make, and the addition of the fresh jalapeño gives it a real kick.

MAKES 4

4 TEASPOONS AGAVE SYRUP, plus extra for the glasses

200ML (7FL OZ) TEQUILA

100ML (3½FL OZ) TRIPLE SEC (we like Cointreau)

80ML (2¾FL OZ) LIME JUICE

ICE CUBES

To decorate

1 TABLESPOON SMOKED SEA SALT FLAKES

1 JALAPEÑO, sliced

1) Brush the rims of 4 short glasses with agave syrup. To decorate the glasses, scatter the salt on to a small plate, then dip the rims of the glasses into the salt so it sticks.

2) Pour the tequila, triple sec, lime juice and agave into a cocktail shaker and add some ice cubes. Shake hard and strain into the prepared glasses.

3) Decorate each drink with jalapeño slices.

EASY MENU IDEAS

SPEEDY THREE-COURSE MEAL

⋯⟩ **SALMOREJO WITH CUCUMBER SALSA** (see page 68)

⋯⟩ **SALT & PEPPER TOFU** (see page 93)

⋯⟩ **SMASHED CUCUMBERS** (see page 155)

⋯⟩ **MOCHA POTS** (see page 190)

PICNIC

⋯⟩ **WALNUT COURGETTE ROLLS** (see page 43)

⋯⟩ **BAGELS & SCHMEARS** (see pages 25–8)

⋯⟩ **SPINACH & PINE NUT FILO PIE** (see page 109)

⋯⟩ **POTATO & GREEN CHILLI PARATHA PUFFS** (see page 128)

⋯⟩ **BUTTERMILK RANCH SLAW** (see page 156)

⋯⟩ **DARK CHOCOLATE CHIP & SEA SALT COOKIES** (see page 214)

GET AHEAD

⋯⟩ **CHIPOTLE & RED PEPPER HUMMUS** (see page 45)

⋯⟩ **ZA'ATAR PITTA CHIPS** (see page 162)

⋯⟩ **LEEK & PINE NUT GNOCCHI GRATIN** (see page 113)

⋯⟩ **CRÈME BRÛLÉE** (see page 195)

COSY SUNDAY

⋯⟩ **CORONATION CHICKPEA SALAD CUPS** (see page 65)

⋯⟩ **ASPARAGUS & CHICK'N POT PIE** (see page 99)

⋯⟩ **SAFFRON ROASTIES** (see page 153)

⋯⟩ **GINGER STICKY TOFFEE PUDDING WITH TOFFEE SAUCE** (see page 213)

GARDEN PARTY

┈┈⟩ **PINK ROSE LEMONADE** (see page 226)

┈┈⟩ **FILO-WRAPPED ASPARAGUS WITH ROMESCO SAUCE** (see page 52)

┈┈⟩ **WHIPPED FETA GARDEN PLATE** (see page 61)

┈┈⟩ **PEPPER CHICK'N ENCHILADA ROJA** (see page 118)

┈┈⟩ **FRESH STRAWBERRIES & CREAM VICTORIA SPONGE** (see page 217)

BARBECUE

┈┈⟩ **EASY WATERMELON SHRUB** (see page 230)

┈┈⟩ **BRAZILIAN-STYLE LOADED HOT DOGS** (see page 127)

┈┈⟩ **BARBECUE SWEETCORN RIBS** (see page 49)

┈┈⟩ **SIMPLE IS BEST POTATO SALAD** (see page 146)

┈┈⟩ **PEACH MELBA PARFAIT** (see page 194)

DATE NIGHT

···⟩ **LYCHEE ROSE MARTINI** (see page 233)

···⟩ **GRILLED PEACH & TOMATO SALAD WITH THAI BASIL** (see page 70)

···⟩ **AMBA CHICK'N KEBABS** (see page 72)

···⟩ **LEMON CASHEW RICE** (see page 159)

···⟩ **LEMON PANNA COTTA WITH BLACK CHERRY COMPOTE** (see page 204)

SPECIAL OCCASION

···⟩ **PEA, SPINACH & POTATO BONDAS** (see page 54)

···⟩ **CHERMOULA CAULIFLOWER GALETTE** (see page 139)

···⟩ **SHIRAZI SALAD** (see page 142)

···⟩ **SOFT HERB SALAD** (see page 145)

···⟩ **CHOCOLATE & ALMOND MEDJOOL DATES** (see page 207)

···⟩ **COQUITO** (see page 239)

GLUTEN-FREE RECIPES

We have plenty of gluten-free recipes for you to enjoy, and for those recipes that require ingredients substitutes, we have included them below. When making gluten-free dishes, do double check the ingredients. Items like mustard, gochujang or kimchi are usually gluten-free, but sometimes gluten can be added as a thickener. Plant-based meat substitutes, including seitan, often contain gluten. Plant-based milks and creams, especially those made with oats, can contain gluten. Soy sauce contains gluten, and so must be substituted with tamari. Gluten-free flours can often be substituted like for like in recipes. Gluten-free bread can be used as a substitute in most recipes, but always check if it is vegan, as many contain egg.

BRUNCH

⇢ **CHERRY PISTACHIO PORRIDGE** (see page 16); if made with gluten-free oats

⇢ **PEANUT BUTTER & JAM OVERNIGHT OATS** (see page 19); if made with gluten-free oats

⇢ **RED PEPPER ONE-PAN SCRAMBLED TOFU** (see page 24)

⇢ **BAGELS & SCHMEARS** (see pages 25–8); if made with gluten-free bagels

⇢ **SWEETCORN FRITTERS** (see page 29)

⇢ **TWO-TOFU SANDO** (see page 31); if made with tamari and gluten-free bread

⇢ **TURKISH-STYLE BRUNCH** (see page 32); if served with gluten-free bread

⇢ **KIMCHI GRILLED CHEEZE** (see page 35); if made with gluten-free bread

⇢ **V'EGG MAYO MUFFINS** (see page 36); if made with gluten-free muffins

⇢ **TEMPEH BLT CIABATTA** (see page 37); if made with tamari instead of soy sauce and served on gluten-free bread

---

SHARING

⇢ **MELON CEVICHE** (see page 40)

⇢ **WALNUT COURGETTE ROLLS** (see page 43)

⇢ **HUMMUS** (see page 44)

⇢ **CUSTOMISE YOUR HUMMUS** (see pages 45–6)

⇢ **BARBECUE SWEETCORN RIBS** (see page 49)

⇢ **TEMPEH LARB** (see pages 50–1); if made with tamari instead of soy sauce

⇢ **PEA, SPINACH & POTATO BONDAS** (see page 54)

⇢ **WHIPPED AVOCADO, JALAPEÑO & BLACK BEAN QUESADILLAS** (see page 55); if made with gluten-free tortillas

⇢ **POTATO & PARSNIP LATKAS** (see page 57); if made with gluten-free flour

⇢ **WHIPPED FETA GARDEN PLATE** (see page 61)

⇢ **CORONATION CHICKPEA SALAD CUPS** (see page 65)

LIGHT

- GRILLED PEACH & TOMATO SALAD WITH THAI BASIL (see page 70)
- AMBA CHICK'N KEBABS (see page 72); check that the plant-based chick'n is gluten-free
- BÁNH XÈO (see page 73); if made with tamari instead of soy sauce
- SPICED TAHINI AUBERINES WITH BRINJAL PICKLE YOGURT & MANGO SALAD (see page 77)
- VIETNAMESE-STYLE PULLED OYSTER MUSHROOM SALAD (see page 80)
- SINGAPORE NOODLES (see page 83); if made with tamari instead of soy sauce
- SMOKY CHICKPEA COBB SALAD (see page 85); if made with tamari instead of soy sauce
- HISPI CASHEW MOILEE (see page 89)

COMFORT

- SALT & PEPPER TOFU (see page 93)
- BOKKEUMBAP (see page 96); if made with tamari instead of soy sauce
- RED LENTIL HARIRA WITH YOGURT (see page 100); if made with rice instead of pasta
- GOMA DARE SOBA (see page 102); if made with tamari instead of soy sauce
- LEEK & PINE NUT GNOCCHI GRATIN (see page 113); if made with gluten-free gnocchi and gluten-free bread
- SAUSAGE & MUSTARD MASH WITH RED WINE GRAVY (see page 114); if made with gluten-free sausages

CROWD-PLEASERS

- PEPPER CHICK'N ENCHILADA ROJA (see page 118)
- BEETROOT TEMPEH SMASH BURGERS (see page 124); if made with tamari instead of soy sauce and gluten-free buns
- BRAZILIAN-STYLE LOADED HOT DOGS (see page 127); if made with gluten-free hot dogs and rolls
- PORTOBELLO & CARAMELISED ONION FRENCH DIP ROLLS (see page 132); if made with tamari instead of soy sauce and gluten-free bread and beer
- PAN CON TOMATE WITH AVOCADO & JALAPEÑOS (see page 134); if made with gluten-free bread
- CHIPOTLE JACKFRUIT TACO SPREAD (see pages 135–6)

SIDES

DRESSING & PICKLES

SWEET

···⟩ **MOCHA POTS** (see page 190)

···⟩ **CARROT CUP CAKES** (see page 193); if made with gluten-free flour

···⟩ **PEACH MELBA PARFAIT** (see page 194); if made with gluten-free biscuits

···⟩ **CRÈME BRÛLÉE** (see page 195)

···⟩ **BUTTERSCOTCH BANANA SPLIT** (see page 200); if made with gluten-free flour

···⟩ **TROPICAL BARK** (see page 201)

···⟩ **LEMON PANNA COTTA WITH BLACK CHERRY COMPOTE** (see page 204)

···⟩ **CHOCOLATE & ALMOND MEDJOOL DATES** (see page 207)

BAKES

···⟩ **GINGER STICKY TOFFEE PUDDING WITH TOFFEE SAUCE** (see page 213); if made with gluten-free flour

···⟩ **GINGER MOLASSES COOKIES** (see page 216); if made with gluten-free flour

···⟩ **FRESH STRAWBERRIES & CREAM VICTORIA SPONGE** (see page 217); if made with gluten-free flour

···⟩ **CHAI MASALA BANANA BREAD** (see page 221); if made with gluten-free flour

···⟩ **FAUX-RERRO FUDGE CELEBRATION CAKE** (see page 222); if made with gluten-free flour

DRINKS

···⟩ **PINK ROSE LEMONADE** (see page 226)

···⟩ **LUXURY HOT CHOCOLATE** (see page 229)

···⟩ **EASY WATERMELON SHRUB** (see page 230)

···⟩ **JASMINE & LEMONGRASS COLD-BREW ICED TEA** (see page 232)

···⟩ **LYCHEE ROSE MARTINI** (see page 233)

···⟩ **PINEAPPLE NEGRONI** (see page 236)

···⟩ **COQUITO** (see page 239)

···⟩ **JALAPEÑO MARGARITA** (see page 240)

GLOSSARY OF UK/US TERMS

AUBERGINE	⟶	EGGPLANT
BAKING TIN	⟶	BAKING PAN
BEETROOT	⟶	BEETS
BICARBONATE OF SODA	⟶	BAKING SODA
BISCUITS	⟶	COOKIES
CAKE TIN	⟶	CAKE PAN
CASTER SUGAR	⟶	SUPERFINE SUGAR
CHICKPEAS	⟶	GARBANZO BEANS
CLING FILM	⟶	PLASTIC WRAP
CORIANDER (FRESH)	⟶	CILANTRO
CORNFLOUR	⟶	CORNSTARCH
COURGETTES	⟶	ZUCCHINI
CRISPS	⟶	POTATO CHIPS
GINGERNUT BISCUITS	⟶	GINGER SNAP COOKIES
GOLDEN SYRUP	⟶	CAN SUBSTITUTE CORN SYRUP
GRIDDLE PAN	⟶	GRILL PAN
GRILL	⟶	BROILER
ICING SUGAR	⟶	CONFECTIONERS' SUGAR/POWDERED SUGAR
PEPPERS (RED/GREEN/YELLOW)	⟶	BELL PEPPERS
PLAIN FLOUR	⟶	ALL-PURPOSE FLOUR
PORRIDGE OATS	⟶	ROLLED OATS/OATMEAL
RAPESEED OIL	⟶	CANOLA OIL
ROASTING TRAY	⟶	ROASTING PAN
SELF-RAISING FLOUR	⟶	SELF-RISING FLOUR
SIEVE	⟶	FINE MESH STRAINER
SPRING ONIONS	⟶	SCALLIONS
STOCK	⟶	BROTH
TEA TOWEL	⟶	DISH TOWEL
TENDERSTEM BROCCOLI	⟶	BROCCOLINI
TOMATO PURÉE	⟶	TOMATO PASTE

INDEX

AUTHOR BIOGRAPHIES

Sarah Wasserman came up in the hippy wholefood scene in the US from North Carolina to Colorado before returning to her roots in London. Sarah cooked her way through art school until she noticed a cool little vegetarian restaurant called Mildreds while completing her studies at the Royal Academy of Art. The anarchic staff and management and creative international menu was a perfect outlet for Sarah's creativity. Sarah has poured her heart and soul into Mildreds, staying with the business as it has grown and changed over the last 15 years. She is the co-author of the two previous cookbooks, *Mildreds: The Cookbook* and *Mildreds Vegan*. She developed the concept and the menu for Mildreds' sister restaurant, Mallow. She looks forward to all the adventures still to come.

Alessandra Malacarne began her culinary career in South Tyrol in northern Italy at the age of 19, under the lead of the 2 Michelin Star chef Paul Schrott. She then returned to her place of birth in Tuscany to work at the 2 Michelin Star restaurant Il Piccolo Principe under the lead of Giuseppe Mancino. Fascinated by different food cultures, she decided to move to London, where she found herself at home. There she could explore different types and styles of cooking, taking her food obsession to the next level. Her first job in London was with the Salt Yard Group under then executive chef Ben Tish. She then moved to Locanda Locatelli. After that, she decided to take a more sustainable approach in life and began work for Mildreds, where she grew from chef de partie to development chef within four years. *Mildreds Easy Vegan* is her first book.

ACKNOWLEDGEMENTS

Thank you to all the passionate Mildreds team and especially the chefs who helped to bring this book into being: Amber-Jean Neale, Sylvia Scordo and Cedrick Payawal. Thank you to Natalie, Yasia and, of course, Sam, for trusting and supporting us. Finally, a huge thank you to David Loftus for your amazing photographs and for being an all-round classy guy.

Mildreds

First I would like to thank Ale for her enthusiasm and inspiration. I would also like to thank my lovely parents, Dr Mary Michael and Martin Michael. And of course, my little gang, Nico, Ari and Neta.

Sarah Wasserman

I have to start by thanking Sarah, who gave me this opportunity. Working with her on the book has been extremely fun and positively challenging. I want to give a special thanks to my London family, Maria Elena and Milko, who pushed me to improve myself every time. My girlfriend Ariadna, who sampled the majority of the recipes with me and has always been supportive. My mum and sister who, although in a different country, are always by my side. And finally my dad, who passed his passion for food to me.

Alessandra Malacarne